Cambridge El

Elements in Politics and Society in Latin America
edited by
Maria Victoria Murillo
Columbia University
Tulia G. Falleti
University of Pennsylvania
Juan Pablo Luna
The Pontifical Catholic University of Chile
Andrew Schrank
Brown University

FEMINISMS IN LATIN AMERICA

Pro-choice Nested Networks in Mexico and Brazil

Gisela Zaremberg
Latin American Faculty of Social Sciences (FLACSO)–Mexico
Debora Rezende de Almeida
University of Brasilia

Shaftesbury Road, Cambridge CB2 8EA, United Kingdom

One Liberty Plaza, 20th Floor, New York, NY 10006, USA

477 Williamstown Road, Port Melbourne, VIC 3207, Australia

314–321, 3rd Floor, Plot 3, Splendor Forum, Jasola District Centre, New Delhi – 110025, India

103 Penang Road, #05–06/07, Visioncrest Commercial, Singapore 238467

Cambridge University Press is part of Cambridge University Press & Assessment, a department of the University of Cambridge.

We share the University's mission to contribute to society through the pursuit of education, learning and research at the highest international levels of excellence.

www.cambridge.org
Information on this title: www.cambridge.org/9781108825962

DOI: 10.1017/9781108919258

First published 2022

A catalogue record for this publication is available from the British Library.

ISBN 978-1-108-82596-2 Paperback
ISSN 2515-5253 (online)
ISSN 2515-5245 (print)

Feminisms in Latin America

Pro-choice Nested Networks in Mexico and Brazil

Elements in Politics and Society in Latin America

DOI: 10.1017/9781108919258
First published online: October 2022

Gisela Zaremberg (she, her, hers)
Latin American Faculty of Social Sciences (FLACSO)–Mexico

Debora Rezende de Almeida (she, her, hers)
University of Brasilia

Author for correspondence: Gisela Zaremberg, gisezar@flacso.edu.mx, Debora Almeida, deboraalmeida@unb.br

Abstract: This Element analyzes the features of current feminist movements in Latin America and their responses to conservative reactions. For this, it focuses on the pro-choice movement vis-à-vis the antiabortion countermovement in Mexico and Brazil. It offers a relational approach, embracing the dynamics within the feminist field and between feminism and the state to capture the movements' potential effects. First, the Element proposes the concept of nested feminist networks, which comprises three dimensions, revealing the plurality of the movement across intersectional and sexual identity issues (horizontal), its relationship with the multifaceted state (vertical), and the intermediation of political parties and participatory institutions in this relationship (intermediary). Second, it argues that nested networks allow feminists to enable policies and block actions from conservatives. In sum, it explores how feminists, leveraging their plurality and connection with the state, can counter conservative attacks.

This Element also has a video abstract: www.cambridge.org/Politics and Society in Latin America_ Zaremberg_abstract

Keywords: feminism, movements, nested networks, conservatives, abortion

ISBNs: 9781108825962 (PB), 9781108919258 (OC)
ISSNs: 2515-5253 (online), 2515-5245 (print)

Contents

Introduction

Feminism is a vigorous movement spreading worldwide. In Latin America, achievements made by a progressive feminist movement include the extension of political rights for women, the enactment of laws against gender-based violence, and the design of reproductive health programs. The extensive protests held in recent years against sexual harassment and femicide, and in favor of abortion rights attest to the movement's renewed vitality on the streets and digital media platforms. These moments, however, are simultaneously threatened by new autocratic tendencies led by religious and nonreligious conservative countermovements. This Element explores how feminists, taking advantage of their plurality, are able to counter these conservative attacks.

The Element has two goals. First, it analyzes the features of current feminist movements in the region, particularly in Mexico and Brazil. Second, it examines how the dynamics of different movements have responded to conservative threats. To address this second goal, we focus on the pro-choice feminist movement in relation to conservative antiabortion reactions in Mexico and Brazil from 2000 to 2018 (and include highlights from after this period). Specifically, we ask: what does the landscape of feminism in the region look like? What are the current central conflicts and points of convergence in Mexico and Brazil? What dynamics enable this movement to best respond to attacks from conservatives in these countries? We provide a conceptual and analytical answer based on the idea of nested feminist networks.

We argue that in Mexico, a more elite and fragmented network, well nested within the three government branches (executive, legislative, and judiciary) and connected to a multi-party nondoctrinal political coalition, enabled a progressive pro-abortion law in the capital city (in 2007), but faced crucial obstacles when dealing with the antiabortion backlash from conservatives at the subnational level in the ensuing eleven years. Within the context of a transformed party system, top-level embeddedness in the judiciary, and a new generation of leadership in both classic and new organizations, this network has only recently achieved more pro-choice results. In comparison, a more cohesive and pluralistic network in Brazil, focused on the executive and left-wing parties, and coordinated across the country, was unable to pass a pro-abortion law but was skilled at blocking conservative attacks. In sum, an elite, fragmented, pro-choice network achieved enabling progress, but was not able to block the backlash at subnational level until 2018, while a more horizontal, pluralistic network experienced major enabling defeats but was successful in blocking attacks.

The first part of this Element (Sections 1 and 2) provides an analytical description of the heterogeneity of feminism – or rather feminism(s) – in Latin America, more specifically in Mexico and Brazil. We critically assess the commonly held idea that feminism has occurred in four waves, with respective periods, agendas, repertoires, and actors. It is commonly assumed that the greatest pluralization of the feminist movement is found in the fourth and most recent, wave, with the inclusion of renewed expressions of feminism and repertories of action (Varela, 2019). These new expressions have been seen in campaigns such as *#Ni una menos* (Not One Less), *Marea Verde* (Green Tide), and different regional derivations of the #MeToo movement. This latest feminist wave is highly critical of the previous generation (usually called hegemonic feminism), specifically of its supposed preference for acting within the state, and inclusion of mainly white, middle-class, educated women, NGO members, and femocrats (Gargallo, 2006; Hooks, 2017). This predominant expression of feminism may have ignored intersectional, transversal, and multidisciplinary boundaries between gender, race, and class; the voices of Indigenous and Afro-Latin American women were especially disregarded (Crenshaw, 1989; Hernández Castillo and Suárez Navaz, 2008). Simultaneously, lesbian, gay, bisexual, and transgender+ (LGBT+) movements have pushed for the transformation of the sex-binary paradigm, denouncing the nonrecognition of fluid sexualities (Careaga and Cruz, 2004).

From our point of view, this perspective of feminism as occurring through historical waves allows us to identify important shifts within the feminist movement over time; but it also hides crucial nuances and offers a simplistic image of a movement that is actually more complex and vibrant (Paradis and Matos, 2013). First, such a characterization of the movement conceals the recurring conflicts across generations. For example, conflicts between pro-institutional and anarchist feminism have existed from the beginning of the movement until the present day. Disagreements over the degree of autonomy the movement should have with respect to governments, expressed in terms of "betrayals versus loyalties" or "true versus false" feminism, have been present in every generation of feminists, as is the case with other social movements. Second, in their lifetime, an individual activist may well experience being both inside and outside institutional or movement spaces (Banaszak, 2010). Third, history does not advance in a straight line. There is no reason to assume that one generation of social movement activists will be completely replaced by another. A whole generation should not be defined – nor distinguished from others – by whether it is perceived as more or less institutionally driven, binary, or intersectional (Sorj, 2016).

We agree with historical descriptions that, unlike the wave approach, depict the feminist movement as intrinsically heterogeneous and "mestizo" since its beginnings (Barrancos, 2020), or even that it may be understood as an ensemble (Alvarez, 2014). Although the concept of ensemble (*assemblage*) makes visible the heterogeneity of feminism, it may work better to explain the ephemeral moments of unity of multiple feminisms (Alvarez, 2019).

As we are less concerned with moments of power emergence and unity and more interested in the heterogeneous and multi-situated continuity of contemporary movements over time, we rely on the concept of networks. Some scholars warn that even when not assembled, movements can be part of networks that share collective identities, have a common adversary or conflictive issue, and collaborate through formal and informal interactions (Diani, 1992; Diani and Bison, 2004; Saunders, 2007). The conceptualization of social movements as networks, however, continues the idea of a shared common identity, which fails to account for the different links established between activists and the feminist movement. At the same time, the alternative notion of coalition – presented by Diani and Bison (2004) for those cases where a strong identity is not present – restricts the analysis to instrumental and short-lived forms of collective action.

To provide a more nuanced and analytical description of the feminist movement in the region, we bring together social movements literature, feminist governance theory, and network theory. We offer the concept of *nested networks* – defined as a space of social relationships[1] that alternates dynamically between separation and incorporation of distinct actors into a common set of repertoires. This relationship between actors is nested within the network and is constantly reshaped, like fluid parentheses that fit inside one another. The parentheses are fluid because they can be alternately inserted or disengaged as required. Actors can thus concurrently have their own entity (as a parenthesis) and be within the network. They can be in conflict and in cooperation simultaneously. In other words, we argue that feminism is a flexible umbrella that provides a space for various feminisms (i.e., radical feminism, autonomous feminism, Indigenous or Afro-feminism, etc.), with distinct levels of engagement. In short, our purpose is to offer a concept that captures the movement's multiple inner conflicts and points of convergence, as well as its openness across different governance arrangements (Woodward, 2004; Holli, 2008) and group expressions, such as social movements, NGOs, civil society organizations, informal groups known as *colectivas* (in Spanish),[2] academics, political actors, governments, and international agencies (Keck and Sikkink, 1998).

1 According to network analysis terminology, networks are spaces of social relationship that constitute a graph. Graphs can include several subgraphs or disconnected components; however, they are still part of the same space of social relationship (Harary, 1969).

2 Young feminist activists in Latin-America refer to their organizations as *colectivas*, a plural feminine of the noun *colectivo* that refers to a collective or cooperative organization.

In this Element, drawing on Alvarez's (2014) explanation of the difference between mainstreaming (vertical fluxes between the movement and the state) and sidestreaming (horizontal fluxes within the movement), we argue that analysts should pay attention to three nested network dimensions – horizontal, vertical, and intermediary – that range on a continuum from fragmentation to coordination. We deepen this classification with the analytical framework set out in Table 1.

The horizontal dimension refers to the dynamics within society – the socio-cultural space occupied by actors, organizations, and social movements – and comprises two subdimensions. The intersectionality subdimension refers to disputes arising from different conceptions of inequality – seen either as an issue exclusively related to the contrast between universal women and men or as a broad question following situated variables referring to ethnicity, race, and class (Crenshaw, 1989). In this Element, we investigate the extent to which classical pro-gender organizations are present in the network in contrast to those advocating for black and Indigenous women's interests in Mexico and Brazil. The sexual identity subdimension includes conflicts emerging from the clash between a binary gendered identity and the more fluid performed sexualities, and related to deep theoretical and pragmatic political discussions of biology and culture, which include distinctions between gender and sexuality, bodies and discourses, and material structures and identities (see Section 1). Here, we compare the structural position of LGBT+ organizations – when present – with that of traditional binary organizations.

Table 1 Nested network analytical framework

Dimension	**Subdimension**
Horizontal	• Intersectionality • Sexual identity
Intermediary	• Political parties • Participatory institutions (councils, conferences)
Vertical	• Branches of government • Territory • Population

Note: The table considers the role of intermediaries played by organizations such as political parties and participatory spaces; however, actors located within governmental institutions such as secretariats and ministries may also act as intermediaries between the movement and the state apparatus and its resources in some cases (Abers and Tatagiba, 2015; Zaremberg and Guzmán Lucero, 2019).

Following the literature on state feminism (see Section 1), the vertical dimension analyzes the relationship between feminist networks and the state. We identify three key subdimensions to address the complexity of the state. First, the three branches of government: executive, legislative, and judicial. This separation of powers is typical of any state under a democratic regime. Most national states in Latin America, and specifically in Mexico and Brazil during the period of our analysis (2000–18), follow the classical division of powers in branches, under presidential systems of government. Second, the subdimension of territory. The notion of domination implies that the state is guaranteed control over a circumscribed territory in order to consolidate sovereignty. It assumes that specific governance mechanisms operate at the national and subnational levels. Both Mexico and Brazil are federal states. As we will show, the pro-choice networks' capacity to expand their reach in relation to antiabortion networks across the territory differs markedly in each case. Third, the subdimension of population: in addition to controlling territory, domination entails control over people, the physical bodies living within certain borders, with the state regulating life and death using gendered codes (Segato, 2014). We question the feminists' connection with governmental areas working with marginalized populations (particularly Indigenous, afro, migrant groups) in relation to dominant (white, urban, wealthy) groups.

Rather than operating independently, some of these subdimensions – both vertical and horizontal – interact within a nested network. For example, the feminist movement is more likely to incorporate different types of groups if it is more widely dispersed over the territory – the subdimension of intersectionality (feminists' links with black or Indigenous women) and the subdimension of territory (the presence of feminist networks connected at the subnational level) are thus clearly and deeply interrelated. We consider this interaction in the analysis of our cases. We demonstrate that, on the one hand, when acting in favor of pro-choice issues, the vertical integration of the Mexican feminist network in the three branches of the federal state offers the movement the possibility of better coordinated action than that of the Brazilian network, which is coordinated mostly with the executive. On the other hand, the Brazilian pro-choice network manages to reach intersectional and LGBT+ groups across the territory while its Mexican counterpart was less present at the subnational level and among marginalized groups until 2018.

With the use of network analysis, we examine the structural network characteristics that impact fragmentation versus coordination. More specifically, we observe many subcomponents within the network and identify those that fulfill such a strategic role that without their presence the network would lose connectivity.[3] We also highlight the crucial role played by what we call connecting organizations, which act as a "network of networks" (national fronts with local filiations, state organizations, and issue networks) (Gurza Lavalle and von Bülow, 2015). Overall, we show that the feminist network in Mexico is less horizontally connected than the network in Brazil.

Finally, we address the intermediary dimension. The horizontal and vertical dimensions are connected not spontaneously but rather through the intermediation of political parties and participatory institutions such as policy conferences, which draw together issues supported by feminists from across the Brazilian territory (Matos and Alvarez, 2018). Whether the horizontal and vertical dimensions are more or less connected is influenced by the historical relationship established during democratic transition processes between feminist's movements, political actors, parties, and state institutions.

Feminism and Conservatism: The Cases of Mexico and Brazil

The conservative backlash against feminists has spread in Latin America and elsewhere, associating the feminist field to a threat embodied by so-called "gender ideology" – a threat that endangers what is conceived as the bedrock of society: the "traditional family" (Wilkinson, 2021). In fact, conservatives paradoxically reduce the complexity of feminism to a supposedly "simple" conspiracy theory, according to which feminism seeks to impose a leftist authoritarian revolution disguised by the gender perspective. This conspiracy reveals a perceived threat to an order based on heteronormative assumptions of sexuality and family, which conservatives seek not only to protect but also to promote (Biroli, Machado, and Vaggione, 2020).

The second part of this Element (Sections 3, 4, and 5) focuses on the tension between feminism and the state, analyzing how the different, specific configurations of feminist networks in Mexico and Brazil respond to conservative attacks. The reader may question and object to our insistence on studying the disappointing relationship between feminists and the state[4] instead of the new lively feminist protests against the status quo and the conservative backlash. Indeed, feminists today are at the forefront of social, political, and economic contentious action that is on the rise in Latin America and elsewhere (Alvarez, 2019). However, we argue that there is still a dynamic interplay between the increasing mobilization on the streets and interactions with the state. We take street protests and other forms of mobilization into account, but will do so while

[3] To better understand connectivity measures, see Wasserman and Faust (1994).

[4] For different feminist perspectives on the state, see Kantola, 2006.

considering the movement's efforts to gain access to political institutions. The era of institutional activism (see Abers, 2020; Abers and Keck, 2013) is not over, and hence the relationship with the state is still relevant. Indeed, although less auspicious and innovative, this form of activism is still crucial to opposing conservative actors in Latin America.

To analyze the conflicts between the movements and conservative actors, we resort to the literature on contentious interactions between movements and countermovements – a key element to understanding the conservative backlash phenomenon (see Meyer and Staggenborg, 1996; Szwako, 2014). We acknowledge that the definition of countermovement is much disputed in the literature (Piscopo and Walsh, 2020), especially concerning its identification with an ideological conservative and reactionary position (Silva and Pereira, 2020). However, we adopt a chronological and relational criterion to define conservatives as an organized countermovement in opposition to feminist movements: conservatives are actors currently reacting to the past actions of feminists. In this sense, feminist mobilizations, especially those in favor of sexual diversity and reproductive rights, have triggered a conservative opposition. In earlier periods, feminists can be seen as the countermovement to conservatives, by politicizing and denaturalizing the Christian perspective on abortion, and bringing different perspectives on motherhood and reproductive rights into the public debate.

We thus propose addressing institutional feminist activism as a tripartite relationship (Roggeband and Krizsán, 2020). In other words, when engaging with the state, feminist movements are not acting alone; they are, at the same time, disputing governmental institutions with their opponents. Interacting with the state involves both advancing a feminist agenda and preventing adversaries from taking advantage of the same institutional spaces. It is important to clarify that a specific examination of conservative actors, their agendas, and actions is beyond the scope of this Element, though we do analyze their relationship with the feminist movement and the state. Although we do not offer readers an in-depth analysis of conservative networks, some observations on the main reactions by conservatives and their attacks against feminism and the state are provided.

One of our arguments is that, as feminists dispute the state with conservative groups, they nest around networks "oriented toward blocking or enabling particular policy outcomes" (Hochstetler, 2011: 350). Thereby, to assure a proper consideration of the full spectrum of the movement's potential effects, we recognize that feminists act not only to promote change and create policies at the state level, but also to block countermovement actions and reactions (Hochstetler and Keck, 2007).

Case Study Selection

We have selected two "diverse cases" (Seawright and Gerring, 2008) – Brazil and Mexico – to investigate how feminist networks resisted conservative attacks over a fifteen to eighteen-year period (Brazil from 2003 to 2018, and Mexico from 2000 to 2018). In some parts of the analysis, we add some explorations until 2021. Mexico and Brazil are diverse cases concerning particularly the variable of religiosity during the analyzed period (see Section 2). Diverse cases offer an excellent opportunity to address complex causal relations and generate innovative hypotheses. However, this methodological choice also makes it more difficult to achieve parsimony, and it requires that the hypothesis be tested to avoid selection and confirmation biases (Nahmias-Wolinsky, 2004). To overcome these issues, we developed three strategies. First, to achieve parsimony, we focus on the question of how feminist networks responded to conservative threats concerning one particular doctrinal issue: abortion (Htun and Weldon, 2018). Abortion is a well-studied issue in the literature, with a constant presence in the history of feminism, responsible for generating vigorous reactions from conservative groups. Second, we keep the network analysis simple. We know that for many readers, network analysis terminology can be demanding. With that in mind, after several analytical procedures, we have strategically chosen a small number of measurements that we believe to be instrumental in highlighting our arguments. Third, with respect to hypothesis testing, we accept that our study is more of a hypothesis-generating than a theory-confirming/disconfirming case study. However, we sought to explore whether our new hypotheses can be replicated by other case studies; that is, if they have heuristic value. To do so, we explore recent literature in search of cases to contrast our analytical model with (in Section 5).

Finally, it is important to highlight that Mexico and Brazil both experienced democratic transitions thirty years ago, an historical background that affects social movements' capacity to coordinate with each other and engage with political actors, parties, and state institutions. As a result, in order to capture specific nested network features, historical processes must be considered. Based on our analysis of the Brazilian and Mexican cases, we argue that interactions with the state are beneficial for the movement depending on the historical access to the state the movement has enjoyed, and the type of nested network built during this interactive process. Nested networks create particular trade-offs between enabling and blocking results, allowing the movement to face conservative reactions differently and obtain distinct results.

Organization of the Element

This Element is organized into five sections. Section 1 outlines the current features of the feminist movement in Latin America, identifying the main conflicts and points of convergence around the subdimensions of intersectionality and sexual identity (horizontal dimension) and examining the movement's interactions with the state (vertical dimension), political parties, and participative institutions (the intermediaries). Section 2 applies network analysis tools to describe these features in the Mexican and Brazilian cases. Section 3 focuses on the vertical dimension of the Mexican feminist movement, offering a processual-based argument of how the Mexican nested pro-choice network was relatively successful in the centralized capital city, but struggled to block conservative reactions at the subnational level until 2018. Section 4 addresses the vertical dimension of the Brazilian movement, presenting a nested network that, although unable to advance its agenda, proved strong enough to block conservatives during the studied period. The strategic role assumed by political parties in intermediating between the horizontal and the vertical network dimensions is also stressed in Sections 3 and 4. Finally, Section 5 explores the heuristic possibilities of our analytical framework, and summarizes the main conclusions, highlighting new hypotheses for future research.

1 Feminism in Latin America

Feminism is characterized by sharp disagreements over how to define its nature. While some scholars may describe feminism as profoundly heterogeneous, others suggest the opposite, that it lacks plurality. Accounting for such complexity requires exploring its main features, including its contradictions and points of convergence. As stated in the Introduction, our approach considers feminism as a nested network. This demands simultaneously analyzing moments of coordination as well as the different conflicts that may lead to fragmentation.

1.1 Feminism and Its Adjectives: A State of the Art

Feminism is not the only existing heterogeneous and emancipatory political movement. Good examples of the plurality of movements are found in the internal differences within labor movements regarding tactics, practices, and overall worldview, as well as the environmentalist movement's various identities, adversaries, and goals (Fantasia and Stepan-Norris, 2004; Castells, 2010). Although this heterogeneity is not exclusive to feminism, it is particularly pronounced within this movement, with its several currents, political projects, and perspectives.

The great number of feminisms – including Latin American feminism – is accompanied by a boom in innovative theoretical perspectives. An endless list of adjectives is used before the word "feminism" to mark divisions within the movement. Indeed, feminism seems to have followed a similar path to what Collier and Levitsky (1997) describe as "democracy with adjectives."[5] Liberal, capitalist, institutional, hegemonic, academic, popular, peripheral, pragmatic, postmodern, reformist, pop, digital, social, economic, political, cultural, cis, lesbo, trans, queer, homo, hetero-normed, heterosexual, separatist, radical, anarchist, Marxist, socialist, autonomous, anti-capitalistic, decolonial, global, South–South, Eurocentric, Anglo-centered, eco, vegan, afro, Indigenous, whitened, blackened, Africana womanism, intersectional, real, true, false, and even patriarchal are some of the adjectives that were used by our interviewees.

Some Latin American and Iberian scholars are critically opposed to conceiving feminism as a multiple phenomenon. They argue that the notion of "performing gender" acts as a Trojan horse within the movement as it introduces a radical relativism that dissolves its main political subject (women). Thereby, "feminism is not plural but in a debate" (Valcárcel, 2019: 218). From this perspective, queer theory – prominently associated with the Butlerian deconstructive feminism (Butler, 2004) – blurs the definition of women as political agents and replaces it with a subject that is sexually fluid and cannot lead the feminist fight. Moreover, these scholars repel the definition of feminism as identity theory and maintain that it is only understandable from a political theory point of view (Miyares, 2017). This discussion also includes elaborate works from lesbofeminist perspectives (Jeffreys, 2003). Due to the scope of this Element, we will not analyze this debate in all its complexity, although we will point out there is not a hegemonic position around it in Latin America, where contrasting theoretical approaches and practices around fluid sexuality paradigms exist (Dehesa, 2010; Correa and Parker, 2019).

Other Latin American scholars address the heterogeneity of feminism from a different point of view, particularly through intersectional and decolonial perspectives (Mohanty, Russo, and Torres, 1991; Lugones, 2011; Mendoza, 2014). These perspectives have provided significant contributions to the field, criticizing the hegemonic narrative of the Global North and its attempt to fit all women into the reality of being a white woman, without considering Latin American women's views on domination and oppression based on territory, race, ethnicity, class, and sexual orientation (Espinosa, 2010). They propose to

[5] To capture diverse forms of democracy, these authors highlight that scholars have increased analytic differentiation, adding adjectives to democracy that may lead to conceptual stretching.

change feminism from inside or to "de-colonize feminism" (Hernández Castillo and Suárez Navaz, 2008).

Communitarian feminism, developed among women of the original nations of Abya Yala, deserves a special mention within the decolonial perspective (Paredes and Guzmán, 2014).[6] Indigenous women suffer (at least) double oppression. Within their communities, they receive unequal treatment from their male partners, while outside, they are subject to discrimination and violence from white, urban men and women. As a result of this complex fight with internal and external oppression, Indigenous women have developed a wide range of positions concerning feminism (Curiel, Falquet, and Masson, 2005; Gargallo, 2012).

These intersectional and decolonial worldviews have strongly influenced processes of state reforms in Latin America, such as constitutional reforms in Ecuador and Bolivia (Pacari, 2004; Prieto et al., 2005; Espinoza, 2011) and legal recognition of "normative indigenous frameworks" in Mexico (Sierra, 2008; Hernández Castillo, 2016). These perspectives have also impacted the actions of social movements, and encouraged the appearance of new feminist movements in the region, comprising both Indigenous and rural women, such as the Mapuches women in Chile (Richards, 2002; Cuminao Rojo, 2009), the Aymaras and Quechuas in Peru (Korol, 2016), and several ethnic groups in Central America (Cabnal, 2010). All these movements were affected by the increase in socioenvironmental conflicts in the region, particularly those associated with neoextractivism.

Partially maintaining their critique of these perspectives and, at the same time, reclaiming their racial background, Afro-Latin American feminists are embedded in a revision of the history of the Latin American slavery experience (Lozano, 2010). Under the motto "blackening feminism," Afro-Latin American women have highlighted that gender inequalities are just one of the various fronts in the fight against oppression and domination. The Afro-Latin American movement introduced the concept of racial violence, expanding the scope of feminism in the region. Black feminists have framed the extended experience of rape during colonial slavery as a traumatic event that led to the eroticization of black female bodies. This eroticization still plays a part in the current violence against Afro-Latin American women, while differences between black and white women hinder overcoming concrete inequalities (Carneiro, 2011). The ascription of Afro-Latin American women to images of domestic servants, such as in colonial times, persists and is embedded in cultural, social,

[6] In 2004, the Indigenous Continental Confederation officially adopted the name Abya Yala to refer to the territory where the original peoples settled, known as the American continent. This name, coined by the Kuna people, means "land of vital blood."

and economic forms of oppression that impede social mobility (Carneiro, 2001). The agenda of black women is influenced by this form of racial violence. For example, as slavery barred the experience of maternity by separating infants from their mothers to be sold as slaves, abortion has not been a priority for black women but rather one of several issues related to "reproductive justice" – which includes not only access to reproductive and sexual rights (Gonzalez, 2008), but also the right to fully experience motherhood, that is, to give birth and also raise their children safely.

In sum, Latin America's oppressive history broadens the range of feminist theories and political positions, with feminists increasingly appropriating the concept of intersectionality (Rios, Perez, and Ricoldi, 2018). Identities based on race, class, or sex, once either in competition with one another or secondary for feminist movements, have become a defining category of feminism (Rodrigues and Freitas, 2021).

1.2 Nested Networks: A Conceptual Proposal

Several attempts have been made to conceptualise the heterogeneity of the feminist movement. Multicultural scholars have proposed concepts such as "plurality of self," "multiple antagonisms" (Alarcón, 1994), "feminist hybridity," "eccentric subjects" (de Lauretis, 1990), or "mestiza consciousness" (Anzaldua, 1990) to capture the multiplicity of the movement. The concept of discursive fields (Alvarez, 2014) and the recent idea of feminism as an assemblage are other examples of these efforts (Alvarez, 2019). As stated in the Introduction, we propose the concept of nested networks to best encompass the multiple and multisituated continuities of the contemporary feminist movement over time, beyond momentaneous protests. In contrast to previous scholars, we offer a concept that is able to capture the political advantages of feminist plurality in the face of conservative attacks. Our proposal is thus strongly based on a theoretical, political paradigm, rather than on a multicultural, deconstructive, discursive, or identity theory. While the plurality of feminism is debatable within these theoretical approaches, our empirical analysis, based on sociopolitical theoretical premises, demonstrates that the plurality of subjects and movements within nested networks is politically relevant for blocking conservatives.

In the fields of network analysis theory and informatics, nesting is defined as incorporating functions or procedures within others by including various levels of parentheses. As will be seen, different currents (e.g. radical feminism, autonomous feminism, Indigenous or afro feminism, etc.) can be thought of as parts of the broader feminist field. Examining the networks' components, subsets, fragmentation, and cut points is crucial to describe – in terms of network analysis – the main features of nested networks.

At the same time, the word "nesting" has a qualitative meaning that conveys the sense of giving shelter. Seen through the lens of this etymological meaning, feminism may be perceived as a flexible umbrella that accommodates multiple guests, who, once achieving a common purpose, may choose to either stay together or leave home (as Barrancos [2020] regularly says: to embark on a diaspora). Some guests may stay longer; others may undertake just sporadic explorations. Some may be new guests; while others may have lifetime membership. Some can be considered guests despite not ultimately recognizing themselves as part of the home (as was seen with some interviewed Indigenous and black women). Some may have one foot in and one foot outside the home boundaries (as sometimes indicated by LGBT+ activists), while others may seek to position themselves as gatekeepers of the house. Still others may even desire to become homeowners themselves.

Beyond the technical, theoretical, or etymological (and metaphoric) meaning, we seek to offer a nonnormative conceptualization to capture the dynamism of the movement, its multiple inner conflicts, and junctures. Moreover, we wish to stress that feminists can simultaneously disagree and agree.

Nested networks comprise three dimensions. First, the horizontal dimension shows how the movement's internal dynamics range on a continuum from fragmentation to coordination with regard to the subdimensions of intersectionality and sexual identity issues. As presented earlier, these conflicts take center stage in Latin America. Second, the network's vertical dimension contemplates the relationship between the movement and the state. Third, the intermediary dimension assumes that coordination between various feminisms (horizontal dimension) and the state (vertical dimension) does not occur spontaneously but is mediated by organizations. The subdimensions of intersectionality and sexual identities were described in the previous section. Here we discuss the other two dimensions (vertical and intermediary).

Over the past twenty years, the literature on civil society and social movements has challenged a dichotomized conception of the state and civil society as two distinct, opposed fields. Contrary to mainstream understandings of social movements based on contentious repertoires (Tilly, 1995), this literature blurs the distinction between incumbents and challengers, and institutionalized and noninstitutionalized politics (Goldstone, 2003; Bereni, 2021), and shows how social actors achieve their goals by working within the state apparatus (Abers and von Bülow, 2011). In their relationship with the state, movements resort to repertoires of diversified actions, ranging from typical contentious actions (marches, protests, boycotts, strikes, etc.) to collaborative strategies, which include proximity politics (personal contact between state actors and society, generally referred to as "lobbying"), institutionalized participation (channels of officially sanctioned dialogue – councils, committees, etc.), and institutional activism (social movements occupying bureaucratic positions) (Abers, Serafim, and Tatagiba, 2014).

Feminist and gender studies offer a plethora of academic research on the relationship between social movements and states. Particularly notable among the extensive literature on feminist governance and state feminism is the concept of femocracy, coined to describe the crucial role of women who moved from the feminist movement into the realm of government (Eisenstein, 1996). The concept has inspired Latin American research (Zaremberg, 2007; Abers, 2020). Other scholars use several triangular notions concerning women's cooperation in feminist governance, such as strategic partnerships (Halsaa, 1998), triangles of empowerment (Vargas and Wieringa, 1998), and velvet triangles (Woodward, 2004). This geometry usually involves three vertices: women politicians, civil servants, and movement activists. Arguing that the use of this triangular framework has the effect of analytically separating feminist politicians and femocrats from the women`s movement, Banaszak (2010) proposes dissolving the dichotomy between feminist "insiders" and "outsiders" to the state. From a comparative perspective, McBride and Mazur (2010) question whether, how, and why women's policy agencies in thirteen countries have been effective in providing the women's movement with inside access to policy-making processes.

The relational approach to the state–society interaction also acknowledges the deeply fragmented nature of the state. Following Jessop (2015), the state can also be understood as a polymorphous institutional ensemble, the different facets of which, although fragmented, are perceived as a unit that dominates. Permeated by interorganizational networks, the state thus performs the dual functions of using the legitimate monopoly of violence and exerting infrastructural power to implement policies across the territory (Mann, 1984).

Based on this framework, we offer three contributions to the literature on state feminism. First, consistent with the literature on advocacy networks (Keck and Sikkink, 1998), we argue that it is important to consider both the informal tactics employed by activists – information politics, symbolic politics, and litigation, among others – and their formal relationship with the state – expressed in women's activism within governmental agencies (femocracies and institutional activists) and the legislative and judicial branches. While the studies on state feminism often focus on activism in one of these branches, we concentrated our analysis on the conflicts arising from the formal and informal relationship between movements and all the branches of power.[7]

Second, network analysis allows us to approach the state–society relationship in its complexity, considering not only the plurality of networks within the movement (horizontal dimension), but also its relationship with distinct state subdimensions (vertical dimension: branches, territory, and population) and their intermediaries. Regarding the intermediary dimension, by taking into account the different historical relationships between political parties and feminist movements and the development of participative institutions in each country, we reach a better understanding of why feminists resort to different strategies for accessing the state.

Third, in addition to examining the three network dimensions, we consider the relationship between different feminist networks and their results in confronting conservatives. Several studies show that social movements are effective at initiating change in distinct phases of the policy process (Kingdom, 1995; Carlos et al., 2017), in varied political institutions (such as state bureaucracies, political parties, and legislatures), and even in different regimes (Amenta et al., 2010; Bosi, 2016; Banaszak and Whitesell, 2017). Beyond influencing results, movements are sometimes able to create "institutional fits" within the state (different access points for influence) and secure "agency domains," that is, "institutional sedimentation" that allows actors to direct the selectivity of political institutions to their advantage (Gurza Lavalle et al., 2018).

We propose slightly shifting the focus of the literature on movements' effectiveness, adopting a tripartite perspective that recognizes the crucial role played by the feminist movement, the state, and conservative countermovements in advocacy processes (Roggeband and Krizan, 2020). Feminists are not alone in dealing with the state; on the contrary, they dispute this space with countermovements. With this perspective in mind, we highlight two simultaneous potential effects of nested feminist networks: (1) enabling equal rights policies to transform the status quo and (2) blocking the approval of conservative policies. Drawing on the tripartite approach, we argue that, when confronting conservatives, feminist nested networks can switch from blocking to enabling functions over time, rather than engage in a struggle between blocking and enabling coalitions (Hochstetler, 2011).

In short, the relational perspective provides us with the tools to analytically describe the heterogeneity of the feminist movement in Mexico and Brazil. It also has implications for the analysis of the dependent and independent variables.

[7] Although Abers (2020) proposes analyzing diverse locations in state institutions and movement networks to understand the groups' access to different combinations of institutional and relational resources, the study is still centered on arenas within the executive branch.

The feminists' ability to enable policies or block conservative countermovements on a doctrinal issue (dependent variable) needs to be situated in a tripartite vision of the relationship between feminism, the state, and conservative actors. Moreover, the feminists' capacity to confront conservatives is dependent on the combination of horizontal (intersectional and sexual identity), vertical (branches of power, territories, and population), and intermediary dimensions of nested networks. The effectiveness of feminist networks is also informed by the historical nature of the interactive process that includes elective affinities between initial ways of accessing the state and particular feminist nested networks.

1.3 Empirical and Methodological References

Gender equality comprises many connected and complex issues. In accordance with Htun and Weldon (2018), the following dimensions and subdimensions may be considered when addressing gender-related policies: (1) "whether a policy empowers all women as a status group or addresses class inequalities" and (2) "whether or not the policy challenges religious doctrine or the codified tradition of a major cultural group" (Htun and Weldon, 2018: 209). Considering our tripartite approach to feminism in Mexico and Brazil, we focus on abortion, an issue that is both gender-status-based (1) and doctrinal (2), and most challenges society's dominant religious doctrine and moral values.

To examine the feminist networks built around the issue of abortion, we conducted a comparative analysis over a period of fifteen to eighteen years (Brazil from 2003 to 2018 and Mexico from 2000 to 2018), together with in-depth interviews conducted between 2017 and 2020 – thirty-three in Mexico and forty-two in Brazil (seventy-five in total; see Annex).[8] Our sample selection included at least two paradigmatic representatives of a particular subset – a parenthesis in terms of nested networks – of the feminist movement in each country. To delineate these subsets, we relied on secondary information and literature to create an initial characterization of the landscape of feminism in each country. We then asked the interviewees to identify the existing feminist currents in their country (survey available in the Annex). Based on the first answers, we used a snowball technique to cover the main heterogeneities. In the Brazilian case, we conducted fifteen more in-depth interviews with politicians and former participants of the National Women's Rights Council, which were

[8] Interviews are referred to by a code beginning with "I" (meaning interview) and followed by a number, to preserve anonymity. Brazilian interviews are identified by codes I1 to I57, and Mexican by codes I58 to I95. This Element's Annex, which includes the acronyms, interview list, survey, and network analysis measures, is available online: www.cambridge.org/download_file/1030418

used to understand the relationship between feminists, participatory arenas, and the legislature. In the Mexican case, five more interviews were held between 2019 and 2021 to explore the notable pro-choice developments that took place after our period of analysis.

Second, we asked interviewees to name five organizations with which they most interact – a technique known as "name generators" – to capture connections between feminist activists in each country. This technique only captures strong ties between activists. Thus, the absence of evidence of weak ties in our network should not be taken to mean that such ties do not exist (see Granovetter 1973). Despite this limitation, the graphs generated reflect the overall panorama, sufficient to analyze our central questions, complemented by the qualitative in-depth analysis. Based on the interviewees' points of view, two types of egocentric networks were built: a general network and an abortion-based network. From the structural standpoint of a whole network, network analysis illustrates at what point collectives, organizations, and subnetworks (subgraphs) are disconnected, to a greater or lesser degree, from other parts of the network. It also indicates which actors ("nodes" in technical language) act as bridges. Specifically, we are interested in a network measure called betweenness. This measure shows how many times an actor (node) is located between two other nodes that are not directly connected (Freeman, 1977). In other words, this measure indicates a particular dimension of power, referred to as a structural position within the general circulation of the network, in terms of strategic location for intermediation (Burt, 2009).

Finally, the historical comparison shows the importance of time in political analysis (Pierson, 2011). The literature has pointed out conceptual elements referring to events and self-reinforced historical processes, such as critical junctures (Collier and Collier, 2002), decreasing, increasing, reactive self-enforced processes (Falleti and Mahoney, 2015), and the classic notion of path dependence (Fioretos, Falleti, and Sheingate, 2016). In our case, we use the notion of events (including the initial ones) modestly. We argue that the way in which feminists have historically accessed the state affects the kinds of nested networks that are created in Mexico and Brazil.

An elective affinity[9] is found between a specific type of access to institutions in democratic states and specific features of feminist networks. In both countries, the democratic transition improved the feminist movement's access to the state but did so differently. In Mexico, there was a democratic process mainly

[9] The Weberian concept of elective affinity is "a process through which two cultural forms – religious, intellectual, political or economic – who have certain analogies, intimate kinships or meaning affinities, enter in a relationship of reciprocal attraction and influence, mutual selection, active convergence, and mutual reinforcement" (Löwy, 2004: 103).

focused on party alternation, which placed political parties and electoral politics at the center of the political scene accompanied by social movements contentious action. In this context, it is expected of an emancipatory movement to prioritize the task of building a robust nested network based on the relationship with the state and occupation of political parties – which ultimately gave the Mexican movement more elective positions within the legislature. Moreover, women's interparty consensus was prioritized while doctrinal issues remained in the background (until 2018). The opposite occurred in Brazil, where state–society interaction during the democratic transition unfolded with social movements – closely linked with leftist parties and a participatory project – joining the opposition to change the political regime. If democratic transitions offer an opportunity to advance agendas through constitutional reform (as happened in Brazil), substantive topics will occupy the activists' agenda. After experiencing a close, long-term relationship with leftist parties at the local level, and in order to ensure a point of access at the national level, a nested feminist network will most likely target the federal executive when a movement party wins the presidency – as was the case with the Workers Party (PT) in Brazil. Although feminists are not deprived of their agency by the process of elective affinity, they act based on the opportunities open to them, limited by the available information and resources. Once decisions are taken, a process of mutual reinforcement occurs.

2 Nested Feminist Networks in Mexico and Brazil

Mexico and Brazil differ in many aspects that impact the analysis of nested feminist networks. To begin with, we consider the social and political strength of conservative and religious countermovements. According to Latinobarometer, the percentage of people in Latin America who identify as Catholic has decreased by almost eighteen percentage points since 2000 (from 76 percent to 59 percent). Despite this general trend, these figures vary differently over this period in Mexico and Brazil. According to the 2020 census, 77.7 percent of Mexicans declared themselves to be Catholic, above the regional average. Nevertheless, a comparison between 2010 and 2020 reveals increased participation in Protestant and Evangelical churches (from 7.5 to 11.2 percent) and a higher percentage of people stating they have no religion (from 4.7 to 8.1 percent) (INEGI, 2021). In Brazil, this tendency is more explicit: according to the 2010 census, the number of people identifying as Evangelicals increased from 15.4 to 22 percent of the Brazilian population, while those identifying as Catholic decreased from 73.6 to 64 percent. It is estimated that, as 14,000 new Evangelical churches open annually in the country, less than half of the Brazilian population will identify as Catholic by 2022 (Queiroz, 2019).

Brazilian evangelical churches, especially Pentecostal and neo-Pentecostal,[10] have successfully accessed high levels of power and political institutions. The number of Evangelicals elected to the Federal Chamber of Deputies increased from twenty-nine in 1998 to eighty-two in 2018. This growing number of religious legislators led to the formation of a congressional Evangelical caucus in 2003. Furthermore, alliances with Catholic political actors, particularly from the conservative Charismatic Renewal movement, helped raise the political influence of the Evangelical Parliamentary Front and increased the presentation of bills against sexual and reproductive rights (Pérez Guadalupe, 2017). Such alliances are particularly notable in the Bolsonaro administration, with three ministries currently occupied by Evangelical pastors, and the creation of a Ministry of Women, Family and Human Rights, committed to spreading family values, and incorporating the previous Special Secretariat for Women's Policies (SPM).

Although Mexico has norms establishing the separation of state and religion, which date to the Reform Laws of 1859 (reinforced after the 1917 Mexican Revolution), gradual changes have undermined secularism in the country. In 1992, the administration of President Salinas de Gortari promoted a reform that granted religious ministers the right to vote (although not to be voted for), legally recognized religious associations, and expanded the access of religious groups to the media. Another turning point came in 2013, when President Peña Nieto's administration approved the term "religious freedom" (which has a public nature) rather than "freedom of worship" (of a private nature).[11] These gradual changes paved the way for the formation of the Social Encounter Party (PES) in 2014, with a religious basis and agenda, and its participation in the electoral coalition with the National Regeneration Movement (MORENA) for the 2018 presidential election (Delgado-Molina, 2020). After winning twenty-nine seats in the legislature (2.68 percent of the votes),[12] the PES lost its registration in 2018, regained it in October 2020 and once again lost it in July 2021. Finally, new public religious actors (i.e. the National Confraternity of Evangelical Christian Churches [CONFRATERNICE]) now occupy crucial positions within the federal government (Aziz Nassif, 2019). They have also participated in the distribution of the Moral Booklet, a text highly promoted by the president himself to spread traditional family values.[13]

---

[10] Pentecostal and Neo-Pentecostal are religious streams within the Evangelical denomination.

[11] Freedom of worship means the freedom for individuals to worship (or not) as a private decision, while freedom of religion refers to publicly tolerating various theological systems and beliefs.

[12] In Mexico, political parties lose their registration if they fail to obtain at least 3 percent of the votes.

[13] The Moral Booklet was written in 1944 by Alfonso Reyes Ochoa (a Mexican diplomat and writer) and is recognized as one of the cornerstones of conservative culture in Mexico.

Mexico and Brazil also differ in their institutional arrangements, one such difference being the centralizing or decentralizing dynamic of their federal systems. Mexico's federal system comprises thirty-two states and a federal district, currently Mexico City (CDMX). The governmental tiers are distributed between the Union, states, and municipalities. According to Falleti (2010), decentralization processes in Mexico are characterized by disputes between a federal government centered around the president, and subnational state governors, who resist impositions. These disputes involve attempts to impose administrative reforms by the centralized national government, followed by contentious reactions at the subnational level. In terms of abortion, it is noteworthy that Mexican state legislatures have no constitutional impediment to deciding their own legislative criteria over the so-called right to life until 2021. It is also important to mention that Mexico does not have a federal penal code, and thus the depenalization of abortion through legislative transformation of the penal code is the responsibility of each state.

Brazilian federalism attributes political authority to three levels of government: the Union, states (twenty-six states and a federal district), and municipalities. According to the 1988 constitution, administrative and political power to guarantee a broad set of social rights (e.g. health care, education, social assistance) is distributed among these different levels, with civil society participation in the policy decision-making process mandatory in some areas and incentivized in others. However, despite these constitutional provisions, decentralization and participation in public policy is a highly uneven process; in some cases, decentralization coexists with centralization and with different levels of authority. For example, in the case of abortion, the Union has exclusive legislative power, since the right to life is established constitutionally as a fundamental right (Article 5, Constitution of the Federative Republic of Brazil). This centralization creates obstacles to subnational legislative initiatives in favor of legalizing abortion, and pushes feminist activism to federal institutions, especially Congress and federal courts.

Another institutional difference between the two countries refers to their party systems. After a long process of democratization, and until 2018, the political system in Mexico revolved around three main parties: the right-wing National Action Party (PAN), which was closely aligned to the Catholic Church and antiabortion activism; the leftist Party of the Democratic Revolution (PRD), which included the right to abortion in its program and was closely associated with the feminist movement during the country's democratization process, particularly in the 1980s and 1990s; and, finally, the Institutional Revolutionary Party (PRI), the pragmatic, oldest party that hegemonically governed Mexico for more than seventy years. In 2018, this tripartite system was dramatically weakened and is currently dominated by MORENA, led by Andrés Manuel López Obrador (AMLO). The Mexican electoral system comprises a mix of relative majority voting and proportional representation. The latter tends to favor women's access to legislative seats (Norris, 1997).

Brazil experienced increasing institutionalization of its party system between 1994 and 2014 (Mainwaring, Power, and Bizarro, 2018: 165). However, this institutionalization was uneven, evidenced by the high electoral stability at national but not at state level. It is also weak across parties in terms of their roots in society and capacities to build robust party organizations. At the national level, the coalition presidentialism – a combination of presidentialism, federalism, and a multiparty system (with thirty-three registered national parties, most of which are represented in the National Congress) – increases the cost of policy changes (Abranches, 2018). During the period under analysis, these characteristics were reflected in Lula da Silva and Dilma Rousseff's four presidential elections, when, in order to secure a majority in Congress, they were forced to build an uneasy alliance with religious groups and conservative actors, impacting the possibility of advancing progressive agendas (Biroli, 2018).

Within these contexts, different feminist nested networks have developed. The following sections analyze: (1) the main inner features of these networks, (2) the strategic positions of some organizations, and (3) the elements that bring together the different parts of these networks.

2.1 Nested Networks in Mexico and Brazil: Cement, Fragmentation, Components, and Node Attributes

In the qualitative interviews, activists from both countries were asked about what compelled them to join forces, and with whom they had engaged in recent years to advance their feminist agenda and build networks (see Annex).

Gender-based violence was unequivocally the unifying element for network components in Mexico (the cement of nested networks) – with violence not only perceived as something affecting women in general, but also concretely experienced by the interviewees. The interviews with young women from different social backgrounds were saturated with accounts of sexual harassment, rape, and even femicide (within the home, public spaces, universities, etc.). Many of them reported being drawn to feminism as a result of the cruelty that their relatives, friends, and acquaintances had experienced (I65, 66, 67, 68). In all these cases, the women were subject to double violence; that is, in addition to a sexual assault, they were mistreated by the state and state agents when seeking redress – particularly by the authorities of the criminal justice system, such as the Public Prosecutors Office (MP) and the police. In addition, some interviewees of all ages spoke of having experienced violence at different moments in their lives (I62, 63, 70); for example, violence related to criminal groups linked to drug trafficking in connection with male political candidates opposing new women candidates selected through parity rules at the local level (I88). Beyond the central role of violence, other issues, such as abortion, women's political rights, and the recognition of the value of care work, were also mentioned by our interviewees as issues unifying Mexican feminist action. These form part of the issues prioritized by feminism and diffused nationally and internationally.

In Brazil, statistics on gender-based violence do not differ significantly from those in Mexico, although the issue seems to be less central. Furthermore, motives for keeping the various feminisms together differ from the reasons why the women joined the feminist movement in the first place. Interviews highlighted that university and student movements are important access points to feminism for the different generations, especially for young feminists between the ages of twenty and thirty. In addition, this age group mentioned their participation in feminist study groups within political parties (particularly the PSOL) and social movements, as well as access to feminist articles on the Internet and in the media (I28). Young activists also mentioned other personal experiences, such as socioeconomic deprivation, racism, and machismo, in addition to contact with campaigns against sexual harassment, and participation in protests, such as the Feminist Spring and "Ele Não" ("Not Him") – a protest against Bolsonaro's election in 2018. Brazilian interviewees further noted international experiences, including the Green Tide and #MeToo protests. Participation in NGOs, social movements, unions, political parties, and the Catholic Church (in grassroots ecclesial communities) was important for older generations. Although violence may not be the main gateway to feminism in Brazil, it is nevertheless an important issue that unites the multiple Brazilian feminisms, although not necessarily personally experienced by our interviewees. Abortion was as important a mobilizing element for activists as violence, which explains the strength of Brazilian feminist activism against the conservative backlash to this issue (see Section 4). The fight against conservativism is the third element uniting the various feminisms in Brazil, manifesting in protests and actions to protect fellow activists.

Regarding fragmentation, components, and attributes of nested networks, the Mexican network comprises more subcomponents and has a generally more fragmented structure than the Brazilian one, as shown in Graphs 1 and 2:

Analysis of the two graphs reveals Interesting characteristics of the nested networks in both countries. First, the nested network in Mexico is far more

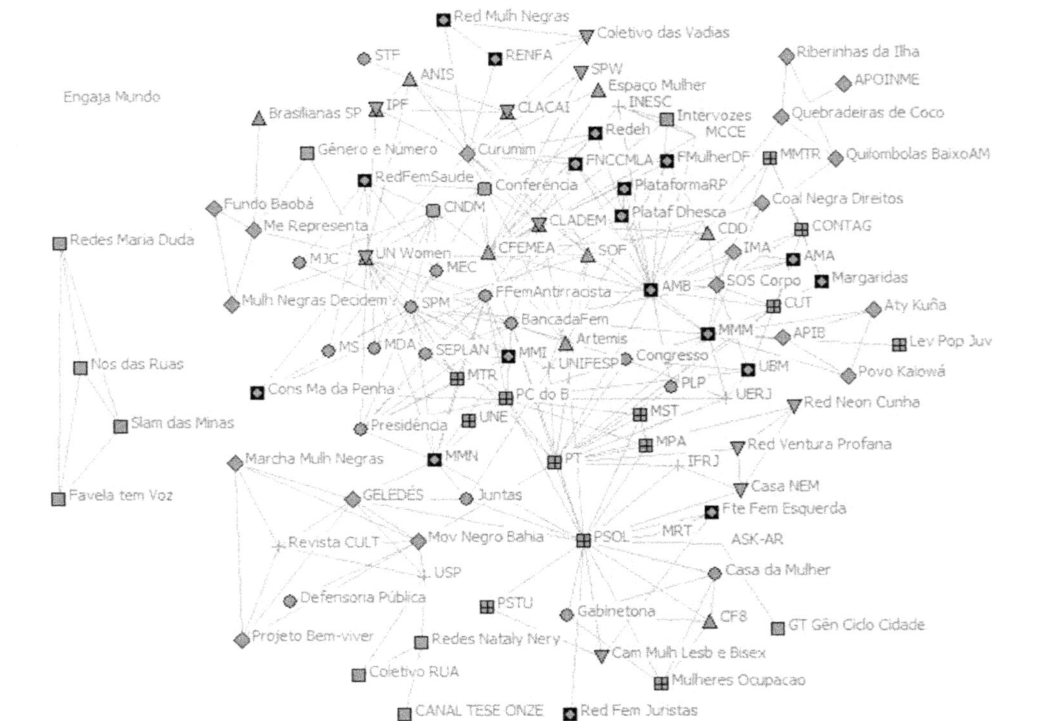

Graph 1 Feminist nested network in Brazil

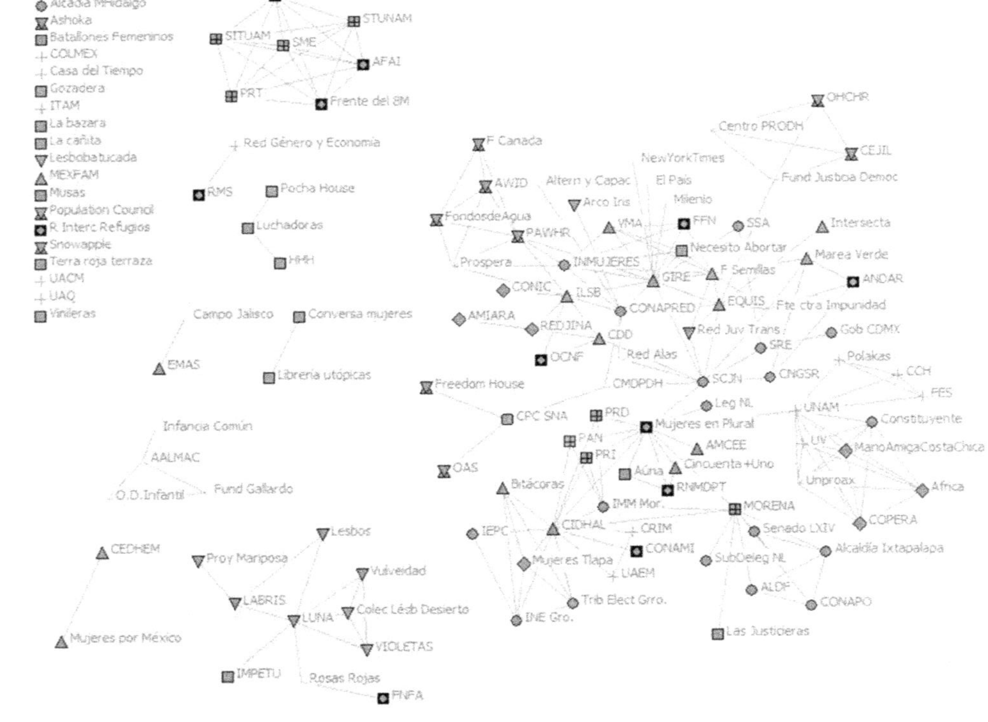

Graph 2 Feminist nested network in Mexico

*Procesed with UCINET. **Circle in a box: connecting organizations; double triangle: international organizations; upward triangle: organizations working on classic gender issues (violence, abortion, political rights); diamond: Intersectional organizations; downward triangle: LGBT+ organizations; square: artistic, mediatic, self-managed organizations, web networks, and collectives; circle: governmental organizations (legislative, executive, judiciary, etc.); plus sign: universities, academic organizations; box: labor unions, corporations, and political parties; rounded square: participative institutions; no shape: others. ***The same legend applies to the rest of the graphs in this Element.

fragmented than the one in Brazil. As shown in Graph 2, the Mexican feminist network has twenty-eight components,[14] including nineteen isolated nodes (nodes with no relationship with each other) that are listed from bottom to top on the left side of the graph. In contrast, in Brazil (Graph 1), only three components are observed, including one isolated node. Fragmentation, as will be analyzed later, signifies less ability to unite forces against conservative attacks.

Second, the multiplicity of shapes shows the heterogeneous composition of both nested networks. Nevertheless, some shapes predominate more in one graph than in the other regarding both intersectional and fluid sexual identity subdimensions. Organizations defending black and Indigenous women (shown as diamonds) are more abundant in Brazil (18 percent [18 nodes in the graphs] than in Mexico (6 percent [7 nodes]). A more careful view reveals that, in Brazil, black women's organizations are more prevalent than Indigenous organizations.

Many factors explain these differences between the Brazilian and Mexican networks. In relation to intersectionality, Brazil was the world's largest importer of slaves and the last country in the Americas to abolish slavery. While Indigenous people suffered extermination in the country (currently representing only 0.4 percent of the population), the black and mixed-race population accounts for 50.9 percent. Black women in Brazil have been organized as an autonomous movement since the 1980s, changing their discursive repertoires and political strategies over the decades in constant connection and tension with feminism over the centrality of race in overcoming women's oppression (Rodrigues and Gonçalves Freitas, 2021). Although during the process of democratization feminism "was not only intellectual, nor white" (I18), there is consensus that the intersectional discourses and practices have only begun to pervade the feminist movement in the last decade.

Our interviews in Brazil confirmed the literature's finding that the introduction of racial quotas in universities created a political opportunity to disseminate intersectional issues (Rios, Perez, and Ricoldi, 2018; Facchini, do Carmo, and Pereira Lima, 2020). The adoption of social and racial quotas in all public universities and federal institutes after the approval of Law N. 12.711/2012 "blackened the face of feminism like never before" (I23). The growing presence of black people and students from public secondary schools (who together account for around 50 percent of students at public universities) expanded the

[14] Components are technically defined as a subset of two or more vertices that are members of the same component if there is a path connecting them.

racial debate into the public sphere and boosted the creation of young black feminist collectives (Rodrigues and Gonçalves Freitas, 2021).

In addition, our interviewees identified the moment that the PT took control of the federal government as key for the incorporation of intersectional issues into feminist networks, especially through participatory spaces organized in different policy areas: "We always say that Black and Indigenous women knocked-down the doors of the conferences. It was the first time they came and hit hard. And with good reason!" (I11).

However, the limited presence of Indigenous movements in the Brazilian network (as shown in Graph 1) was reproduced in the federal government. As a representative from the Indigenous women's movement noted: "It was not enough to approve the proposals of indigenous women in the conferences. It was 'cute' there in the government plan, but in the budget, which represents the real will to carry out the actions, they were never a priority" (I24). The distance between Indigenous people and feminism also derives from the identification of feminism with eurocentrism (and, consequently, colonialism), the struggle of Indigenous people for autonomy, and their different agendas and modes of life (I25). Nevertheless, the nesting process does occur in some contexts, particularly in the fight against external enemies: the state and private actors, regarding issues related to violence, labor rights, and access to political arenas.

The analysis of intersectional heterogeneity reveals that Brazilian networks are better equipped to find common ground amid diversity than those in Mexico. However, various disagreements still exist regarding the agenda and forms of collective action that should be prioritized. As one interviewee declared: "While white women were fighting for the right to work, we were already enslaved" (I26). And another: "Young feminists have the right to the body as their main struggle. For black women, the struggle is to survive" (I17). The critiques are expressed particularly by young black activists, located in the margins of the network, and related to the cultural activism emerging on the urban outskirts (Medeiros, 2019).

In contrast, in Mexico, neither Afro-Mexican nor Indigenous women's organizations are strongly represented in the graph (located in the margins of Graph 2). This is noteworthy given that, according to the 2021 Mexican Census, 9.7 percent of the population are part of an Indigenous group – with women making up 51 percent of this Indigenous population. At the same time, 2 percent of the population consider themselves Afro-descendant or Afro-Mexican – 50.4 percent of which are Afro-descendant women (INEGI, 2021).

Graph 2 shows the presence of Indigenous women's organizations, particularly connected to the National Coordination of Indigenous Women (CONAMI) and Afro-Mexican women organizations (such as Mano Amiga Costa Chica).

However, they are not prevalent in the network. As will be analyzed in Section 3, difficulties in reaching subnational levels and a history of mutual distrust, and even armed conflicts, between governments and Indigenous Mexican movements have hindered better connections between urban Mexican feminism and Indigenous women's movements.

The differentiation between nested networks in Brazil and Mexico in relation to the sexual identity subdimension also deserves attention. Although the graphs show that 7.8 percent (10) of the organizations in Mexico and 5.7 percent (6) in Brazil are LGBT+ organizations (shown as downward triangles), this general classification obscures a crucial distinction regarding conflicts around sexual identities. In Mexico, the majority of these organizations (80 percent) are lesbian nodes strongly holding a separatist[15] standpoint, from which they exclude queer and transgender paradigms, basing their activism on biological arguments. Our interviews with lesbians, radicals, and abolitionist[16] Mexican activists were saturated with this perspective:

> So [feminism] is only for women . . . LGBT is not even ours. Everything that fights for inclusion is not feminist, in reality, it is anti-feminist . . . , it is used to erase women . . . . So yes, there is a very powerful feminism, but it is a feminism that is in danger of believing all those queer stories. (I62)

> The violence that a trans female can experience can be compared to the violence that women experience?! [That] is also a way to tarnish the struggle, a way to silence ourselves, a way to prioritize dissidents over ourselves. (I64)

> It is very logical and easy to observe: We do not think that trans identities represent us or that, if they want, they could be part of our movement . . . We are abolitionists and we do not think that men can be women only because they state it. (I68)

The LGBT+ field in Mexico is thus clearly filled with conflicts. An organization of lesbians may profoundly disagree with another organization fighting for transgender and queer rights (e.g. the right to officially change their identity) while simultaneously opposing an organization working on a classic binary conception of gender. Furthermore, by supporting anarchist and anti-capitalist radical positions, many lesbian activists also argue that queer perspectives legitimate capitalism. In other words: "It is tricky to believe this thing of inclusion. Patriarchy and capitalism are [simulating] the motto of all inclusive. A Coca-Cola commercial is offered for everyone: the patriarchy loves that all

[15] A separatist feminism argues that men and women should be separated in certain spaces in order to ensure women's safety.

[16] Abolitionist feminism fights against the commercial and sexual exploitation of the female body: prostitution, gestational surrogacy, and pornography.

people feel included" (I63). Anti-capitalist positions are also held by other feminisms (e.g. some communitarian feminisms), but not with the same point of view, which differentiates between men and women and excludes fluid sexualities.

Curiously, certain Mexican institutional feminist activists accused of being hegemonic and even patriarchal by some radical feminist respondents from collectives agree that the distinction between men and women should not be blurred. Some institutional activists stress that feminism is not an identity but a political movement fighting for women's rights. Then, for example, gender parity is a right that is based on a binary opposition between men and women. The fight for LGBT+ rights and women's rights are thus two different struggles that must be carefully reconsidered (I87). This caution is not merely abstract but has everyday applications, such as the recent legal disputes over transgender identities and the parity rule (Soto Fregoso, 2019). Some of these institutional activists did not support biologically based differentiations or sexual identity exclusions of transgender people, while others hold these premises. In this context, on January 15, 2021, the Instituto Nacional Electoral approved affirmative action supporting the registration of Indigenous, Afro-Mexican, LGBT+, and disabled candidates.

In contrast, there is less radical divergence between LGBT+ organizations and those working on classic gender issues in Brazil, although conflicts still exist. It is important to state that we tried to interview, without success, five radical feminist groups that are organized online through Facebook. In a brief search on this social media platform, using the names "radical lesbian," "radical feminist," and "radical feminism," we found at least ten active pages. A brief look at the posts revealed the same pattern of critiques of queer and transgender paradigms and agendas found in Mexico, as well as the same anti-capitalist perspective, with transfeminism conceived as a new form of patriarchal capitalist domination over bodies. Based on the idea that Simone de Beauvoir was misunderstood by queer theorists, the Radical Feminism of Brazil Facebook page declares: "Your personality does not make you a woman, the brain is not a sexual organ" (June 29, 2020).

According to interviewees from the lesbian and feminist movement in general, such feminism in Brazil has increased since the Feminist Spring of 2015. It is organized primarily around digital activism, but also within political parties, such as the PSOL, as well as in the form of collectives. Despite this growing presence, the exclusion of transfeminism is opposed by several other activists, who argue that such exclusion restricts women's activism and undermines feminism (I27).

Three points regarding the encounter between feminism and the LGBT+ field should be highlighted. First, the presence of research groups on women, gender, and sexualities at Brazilian universities since the transition to democracy and the growing visibility of queer theory and academic studies on transgender people since the 2000s have contributed to the radical rejection of the pathologization of transsexuality in academia, and have given inputs to transgender activists and other social movements to criticize their opponents (Coacci, 2018). Second, the transgender movement in Brazil has a long tradition of organization dating from the 1990s, and has experienced important shifts over time, including the emergence of a transfeminist field and transgender collectives who collaborate to raise awareness of the transgender issue as a central axis in the mainstream feminist debate. Finally, while the relationship of lesbians and feminism has also been marked by moments of approximation and separation, the growing visibility of lesbian activism – and the activation of intersectional, queer, and decolonial theories at the end of the twentieth century – strengthened the relationship between feminism and the LGBT+ field, even as tensions continue (Facchini, do Carmo, and Pereira Lima, 2020). Finally, the Brazilian Lesbian Articulation has joined national connecting organizations – such as the Brazilian Women's Articulation (AMB) and the National Feminist Health Network – and participated in national conferences.

2.2 Nested Network: Strategical Positions

We have analyzed the strategic positional power of the organizations acting as intermediaries based on the measure of betweenness, which shows the number of times a node lies on the shortest path between two nodes that are not directly connected (Freeman, 1977). The notion of intermediation is conceived as the power to "be in the middle and acting as a means to," which involves some capacity to politically represent interests and demands (Zaremberg, Guarneros-Meza, and Gurza Lavalle, 2017).

Graph 3 shows that, in Mexico, the three better-positioned nodes within the largest component of the network are: (1) Women in Plural (Mujeres en Plural; a connecting organization fighting for women's political rights, represented by a circle in a box); (2) the Supreme Court of Justice of the Nation (SCJN; represented by a circle); and (3) an organization called Information Group on Reproductive Choice (Grupo de Información en Reproducción Elegida [GIRE]; represented by an upward triangle). Graph 3 also resizes nodes based on higher or lower scores of betweenness.

Mujeres en Plural appears 1870.50 times (22.6 percent) in the middle of a shorter path (technically referred to as a geodesic path) between two nodes that

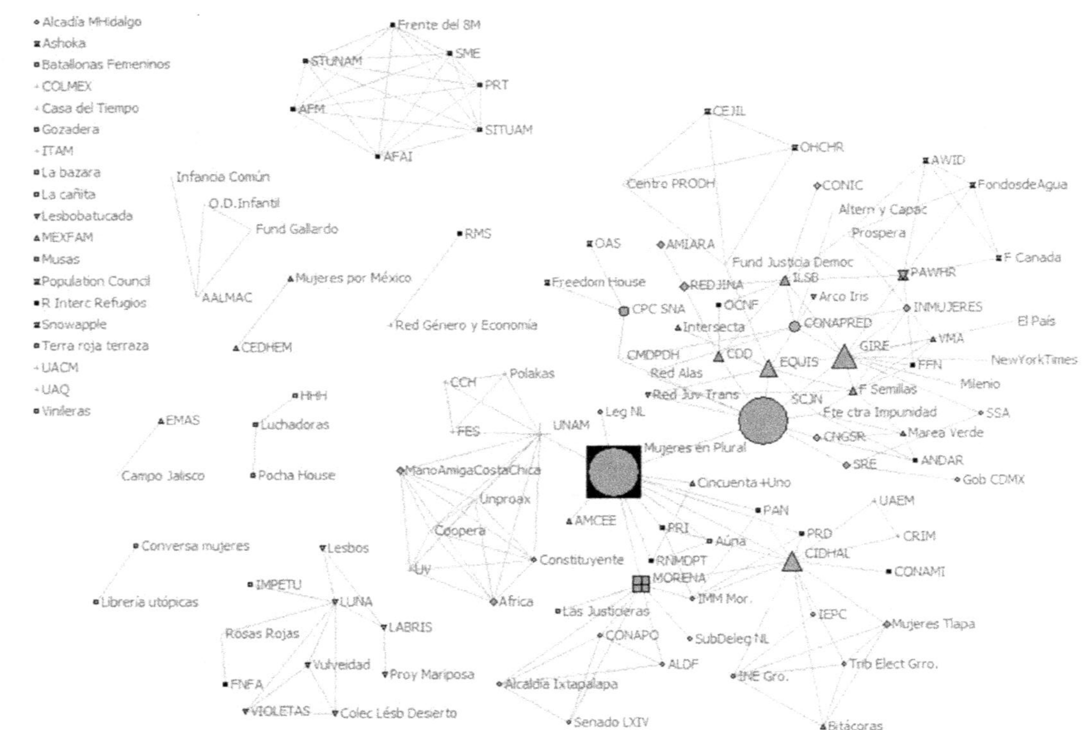

Graph 3 Nested network in Mexico by betweenness

*See Graph 1 for legend

are not directly connected, while the SCJN appears 1726.35 times (20.9 percent) and GIRE 835.33 times (10.1 percent).[17]

Mujeres en Plural and the SCJN are also cut points, meaning that if they were removed from the network, the network would lose connectivity.[18] The central position of Mujeres en Plural was not surprising as it is the most powerful network for advancing women's political rights. Similarly, GIRE is a well-known NGO fighting for abortion rights. While the position of the SCJN may have been surprising in 2019, recent complementary interviews illustrated that this position was related to a renewal of feminist repertoires regarding socio-legal mobilization after 2007. These repertories paid off in the historical pro-choice rulings of the Mexican Supreme Court in 2021 (we will return to this in Section 3.4).

The actors who fulfill this connecting function in Brazil are different. As shown in Graph 4, the most striking difference in the Brazilian case is the role of leftist political parties in connecting the network.

Among the three better-positioned nodes, the PT appears 1223.8 times (22.8 percent) in the shortest path between two nodes that are not directly connected, while the PSOL appears 1210.4 times (22.6 percent). The AMB, a connecting organization, appears 1069.9 times (19.9 percent). The AMB and PSOL are cut points (or articulation points). In particular, if the PSOL were removed from the network, several organizations involved with intersectional and fluid sexuality issues would be disconnected in a separated component.[19]

In contrast with Mujeres en Plural in Mexico, the connecting organization AMB – created in 1994 to organize women's participation in preparation for the Beijing International Women Conference – does not focus on a single non-doctrinal issue. With affiliates in seventeen states, the network connects organizations from across the country in defense of political reform and women's political participation, abortion rights, socio-environmental justice, Indigenous rights, and social security, and against racism and the neoliberal agenda. It has influenced many regional and national policy processes, including the approval of the Maria da Penha Law against gender violence (Carone, 2018). On the other hand, it is noteworthy that the network's configuration was affected by Dilma Roussef's impeachment in 2016. The roles of the PT and the PSOL, for instance, changed dramatically.

---

[17] The average betweenness score of the network is 65.7 (8 percent). The network centralization index is 21.9 percent (See Annex).

[18] A cut point of a figure is a vertex, the removal of which increases the number of components (Wasserman and Faust, 1994).

[19] The average betweenness score of the network is 99.8 (1.8 percent). The network centralization index is 21.2 percent (See Annex).

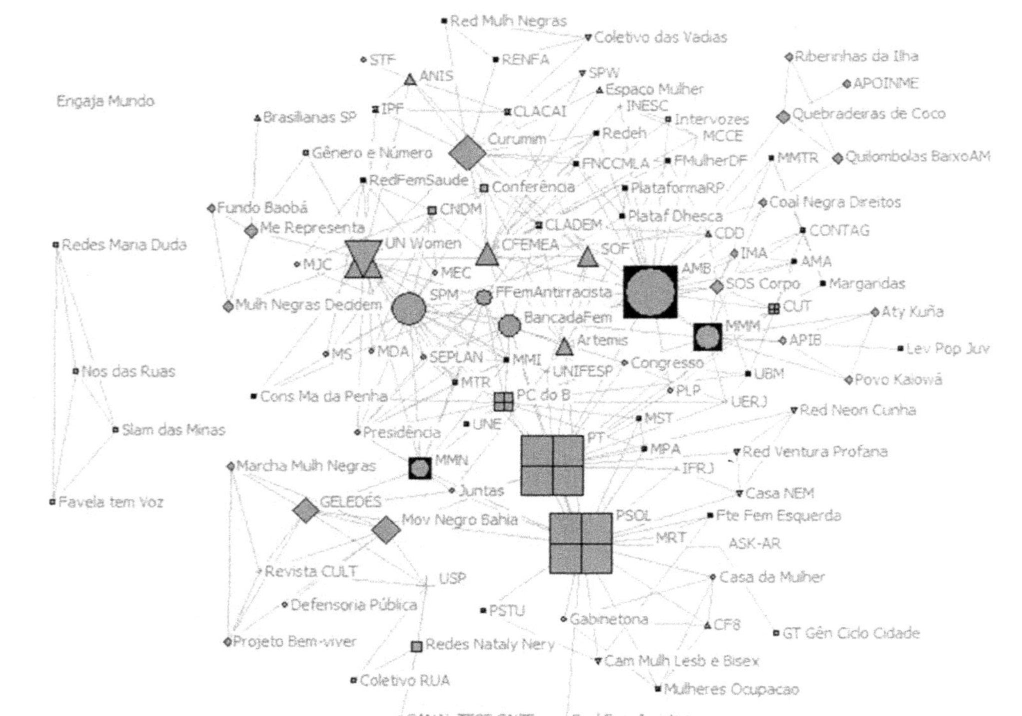

Graph 4 Nested network in Brazil by betweenness

*See Graph 1 for legend

By comparing the configuration of the Brazilian network before (Graph 5) and after Rousseff's impeachment (Graph 6), we see that the PSOL (represented by a box) increased its betweenness score after this critical event. Before the impeachment, the AMB (circle in a box) had the highest betweenness score, closely followed by the PT (box), while the PSOL (box) had a score similar to that of the PCdoB (for numerical betweenness index, see Annex). Government agencies such as the Secretariat for Women's Policies (SPM; represented by a circle) clearly played an important connecting role when the PT was in government. After 2016, the SPM node, as well as the Planning Secretariat (SEPLAN) and other state departments and ministries, disappeared from the network as a result of a major administrative and ministerial reorganization under the presidencies of Michel Temer and Jair Bolsonaro.

The striking growth of the PSOL (box) after 2016 is evident (see Graph 6). The PSOL was created in 2004 by a group of left-wing activists, intellectuals, and former PT politicians, increasing its relationship with the youth, black, Indigenous, and LGBT+ movements since the 2013 cycle of protests in Brazil. The party has attracted different generations of social activists who, although sometimes aligned with the PT, are critical of its past strategies and current political projects. The Anti-Racist Parliamentary Front, which acts in defense of women's rights and against racism (FFemAntiracista;represented by a circle) also appears in Graph 6 instead of the Feminine Parliamentary Group (Bancada Feminina; circle), reflecting the increasing importance of intersectional issues in the network.

As shown in Graph 6, governmental actors (represented by circles) disappeared from the network after 2016. Moreover, the network became more heterogeneous with the addition of new organizations – particularly those linked to LGBT+ rights (downward triangles) and to artistic and social media repertories (squares). Some organizations remained equally present. UN Women (double triangle) and Curumim (diamond) have similar positions in the betweenness index. It is interesting that Curumim, an intersectional organization created in the 1980s to advocate for black women's rights, occupies a strategic position both before and after 2016. This node is also a cut point. The nodes related to Indigenous women's rights, however, reflect their distinct situation. They are not located in any strategic position, confirming their less prominent role in the network, as mentioned previously. It should be noted that in Mexico, neither Afro nor Indigenous women's organizations occupy a central position in terms of betweenness or cut points.

We have discussed here the different features of nested feminist networks in Brazil and Mexico. In the following section, we analyze the different ways in which the Brazilian and Mexican nested networks respond to conservative antiabortion reactions.

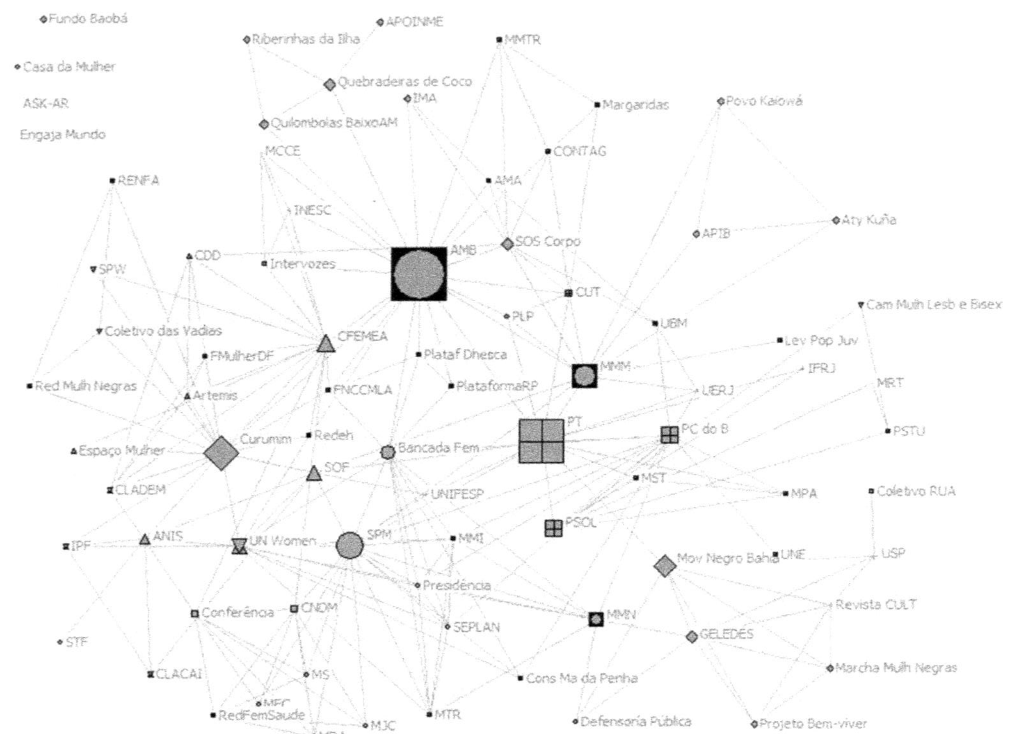

Graph 5 Nested network in Brazil by betweenness before 2016

*See Graph 1 for legend

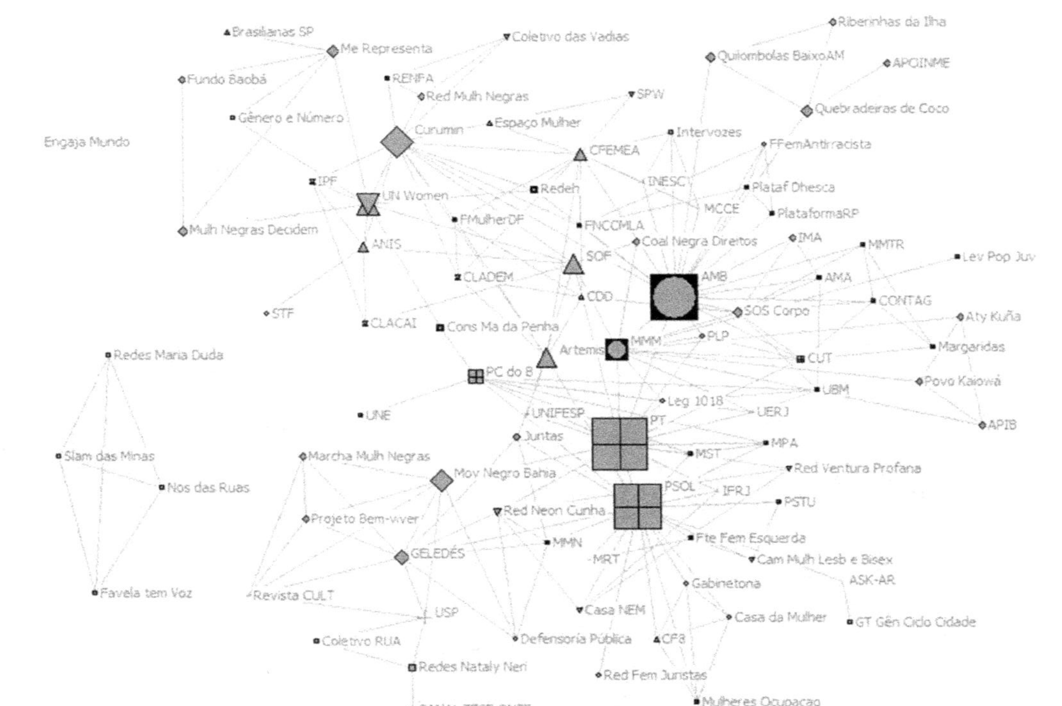

Graph 6 Nested network in Brazil by betweenness after 2016

*See Graph 1 for legend

3 Abortion Rights in Mexico: Feminist Advances and the Backlash at National and Subnational Levels

The Mexican political system is marked by more than seventy years of the PRI's domination and by an extended transition to democracy that lasted until 2000, when party alternation began. Achieving this result had been a goal for political actors during the Mexican democratic transition. Although the feminist movement had played a crucial role in the regime's transition, the alternation of 2000 paradoxically brought to the executive a right-wing party that did not support doctrinal issues within the feminist agenda. In this context, the nested feminist network focused on nondoctrinal issues, such as women's political rights and gender violence, and paid less attention to more controversial topics (such as abortion). This strategy prevents doctrinal conflicts from arising among diverse religious-ideological party cleavages, comprising both the right and the left. In the Mexican case, close vertical coordination between the feminist movement and the three government branches on nondoctrinal issues at the national level thus coexisted with limited horizontal coordination within the movement. This particular arrangement has enabled progress in abortion rights in a centralized location (Mexico City) and facilitated the blocking of conservative attacks at the national level, but, at the subnational level, it inhibited both the support of political elites and the mobilization of massive street protests over this issue until 2018. The historical process of feminist nested networks in Mexico until 2018 is summarized in Graph 7.

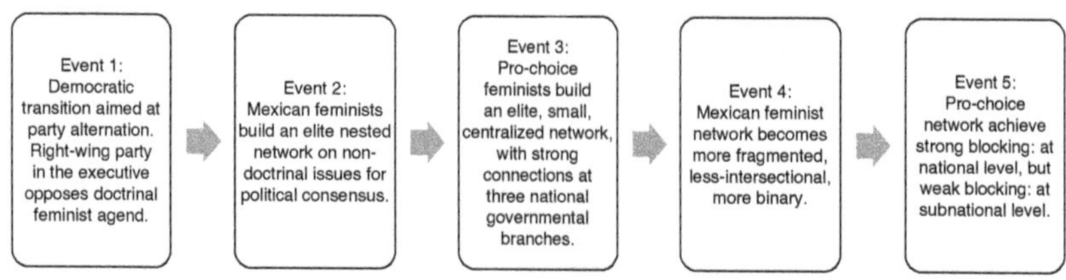

Graph 7 Historical process Mexico (2000–2018)

The next section develops each of the features and events in the historical sequence represented in Graph 7.

3.1 Feminism, Parties, and the State in Mexico until 2018: A Nondoctrinal Agenda

Scholars concur in referring to the Mexican case as undergoing a "prolonged transition" (Labastida Martín Del Campo, and Leyva, 2004). In doing so, they allude to the gradual regime change as "trench warfare" between ruling groups and opposition parties (Schedler, 2010). This process took place over an extended period, which some scholars date from the late 1960s to 2000. During this time, the Mexican democratic transition followed the "obsession" of ensuring party alternation in the federal executive.

The first alternation in power finally came in 2000, when the PRI lost an election for the first time in seventy years, to the PAN. In 2012, after the PAN had occupied the presidency for twelve years, and against a context of accelerated deterioration in democratic conditions and public security in the country, the PRI once again won the presidential election and regained power. Nevertheless, six years later, in 2018, the electoral triumph of MORENA severely transformed the previous party system. MORENA is an offshoot of the left-wing PRD. In addition to a resounding victory in which MORENA secured the executive and a majority in both legislative chambers, the party also won most of the governorships that were up for election in 2018. All twelve states holding legislative elections and controlled by the PRI flipped to MORENA in 2018. In the Federal Chamber of Deputies, the PRI's representation plummeted – from 204 seats (out of 500) to only 47. In addition to the electoral defeats, a corruption scandal in relation to the past administrations of both the PRI and PAN, created an uncertain future for these parties.

Mexican feminism has been a strong social movement involved in the long democratic transition. In the 1990s, before party alternation, Mexican feminism was remarkably dynamic. As had happened in Brazil (and in most Latin American countries), feminist activism was strengthened by the participation in international women's conferences, and by the inpouring of financial resources from international cooperation agencies (Vargas, 2008). These processes promoted gender mainstreaming within the executive and facilitated access to seats in the National Legislature.

Congresswomen in the 1997–2000 legislature – before the 2000 electoral alternation – played a crucial role in creating the Women's Parliament (WP) in 1998 as an arena for civil society organizations to exchange experiences and build a legislative agenda (Martinez Medina, 2010). This arena, which involved the participation of more than 1,300 activists, was designed to raise public awareness of the women's agenda and respond to legislators' resistance. It resulted in a reform of the civil code and social security system in favor of women's rights. In the following legislature, the National Institute for Women (INMUJERES), demanded by the WP, was created.[20]

However, the democratic transition also produced a remarkable paradox. In 2000, it brought into the executive branch a right-wing conservative party that

[20] This national women's institute was created in 2001.

opposed a substantive feminist agenda. Doctrinal issues such as abortion and sexual and reproductive rights faced vigorous resistance (Tarrés and Zaremberg, 2014). Feminist women started to subtly fight this opposition within the legislative, executive, and judicial branches. Consolidating a basic consensus among feminists and establishing a gender-based agenda within the three main political parties (the PRD, PRI, and PAN) became crucial.

During the 2000–3 legislature, the WP was occupied by conservative organizations proposing policies against abortion and in favor of the family, morals, and religion. Despite various mediation strategies, a confrontation became unavoidable, and so the WP was abolished, hindering the contact between grassroots feminists and political activists. In other words, the horizontal and vertical dimensions became increasingly distanced from each other. It is thus not surprising that feminists resorted to repertoires that were different from those used by previous congresswomen when trying to approve the General Law for Women's Access to a Life Without Violence (LGAMVLV) during the 2003–6 legislature. As shown by Torres Pacheco (2008) and Martinez Medina (2010), the agenda was built by only a few women's rights advocates, who did not spark too much ideological conflict.

Meanwhile, feminist congresswomen increasingly stopped conservative strategies from the executive. A key conflict emerged precisely because of the pro-family profile of INMUJERES's new president (Patricia Espinosa Torres, 2001–6). For instance, the Equity and Gender Commission in the legislature refused to approve resources for INMUJERES, and instead allocated them to other government departments in which pro-gender officials ensured that they would not be used in favor of conservative interests.[21] This counterbalance nested network was built on a consensus on nondoctrinal issues among congresswomen, institutional activists within the federal administration, and feminist activists outside the government. It is not a coincidence that the legislative agenda during this period focused on nondoctrinal issues such as gender mainstreaming, gender budgeting, gender-based violence, and gender quotas (Zaremberg, 2009).

These paradoxical confrontations at the beginning of the democratic alternation of 2000 established a pattern of cohesive, nondoctrinal, feminist institutional activism centered in the legislature but expanding into the executive and judiciary. Although affiliated with the PAN, the second president of INMUJERES, Rocío García Gaytán (2006–12), was a progressive who rebuilt the organization's relationship with gender equality advocates in the legislature.

[21] This occurred with resources to tackle gender violence that were not assigned to INMUJERES but rather, to the National Institute of Social Development (INDESOL) (I76).

Finally, the third INMUJERES president, Lorena Cruz Sánchez (2012–18), a member of the PRI, kept a distance from some activist networks but maintained a positive relationship with congresswomen and senators.

In this context, unsurprisingly, Mujeres en Plural was created in 2009 as one of Mexico's most potent connecting networks to achieve gender parity. It is a "network of networks" composed of women with extraordinary trajectories within the government, the feminist movement, and academia. Our interviewees recognize Mujeres en Plural as a key actor in issuing the ruling of 30 November 2011, which sanctioned political parties for neglecting the gender quota law. This case attests to the electoral judiciary's strong support for the enactment of the quota law, which had faced several obstacles despite reforms in successive legislatures. It was only possible to fully overcome these obstacles because of the synergy between feminists and the judiciary.

In 2014, the same nested network guaranteed that gender parity became a constitutional principle. In 2019, it promoted and approved another constitutional reform called "parity in all," which made parity in the three branches of government at the federal, state, and municipal levels constitutionally mandatory, protecting women's right to equally participate in all political spaces with men. Gender parity applies to political parties, independent bodies, and any entity or body with authority at the national or subnational level. In 2020, this network was responsible for reforming eight general laws (including the LGAMVLV), creating a legal framework to combat political gender violence against women. Finally, in 2021, it pushed for new affirmative action to reserve candidacies for Indigenous, sexually diverse, disabled, and migrant people. This set of reforms makes Mexico one of the most progressive countries regarding women's political rights.

However, these achievements required building a broad internal consensus within the nested network, particularly regarding abortion issues. As one of our interviewees says:

> They [Mujeres en Plural] take great care of that [the consensus], obviously because there are issues, let's say, that are not accepted very easily . . . if you allow me, the collective imagination of this, it is the issue of abortion . . . So, something that has worked very well for them is to keep the subject very encapsulated. This is called women's political participation and let's not go further because then, we lose the consensus. (I87)

This clearly reveals the logic of Mujeres en Plural in not including doctrinal issues that left- and right-wing women cannot agree on within one of the most important connecting nodes of the feminist nested network in Mexico.

3.2 Elite, Isolated Pro-choice Nested Network

Until 2018, the Mexican pro-choice network shared some elite features with the connecting organization Mujeres en Plural. Highly educated women are at the center of this network, with notable connections to international cooperation organizations, public officials within the three branches of government, and mainstream media journalists. Like Mujeres en Plural, it is an issue-based network but focuses on abortion and women's sexual and reproductive rights, maintaining poor relations with intersectional and LGBT+ organizations. Contrary to Mujeres en Plural, however, it is badly connected with the subnational level, and has no direct links with political parties, relying on contacts with leading women politicians. Their relationships with these women leaders had moments of convergence, but also serious disagreements whenever conservative reactions at the subnational level challenged the nondoctrinal consensus that women politicians had built. As will be analyzed in this section, this small and cohesive pro-choice network (shown in Graph 8) was relatively effective in blocking antiabortion reactions at the federal level; however, it struggled to do the same at the subnational level.[22]

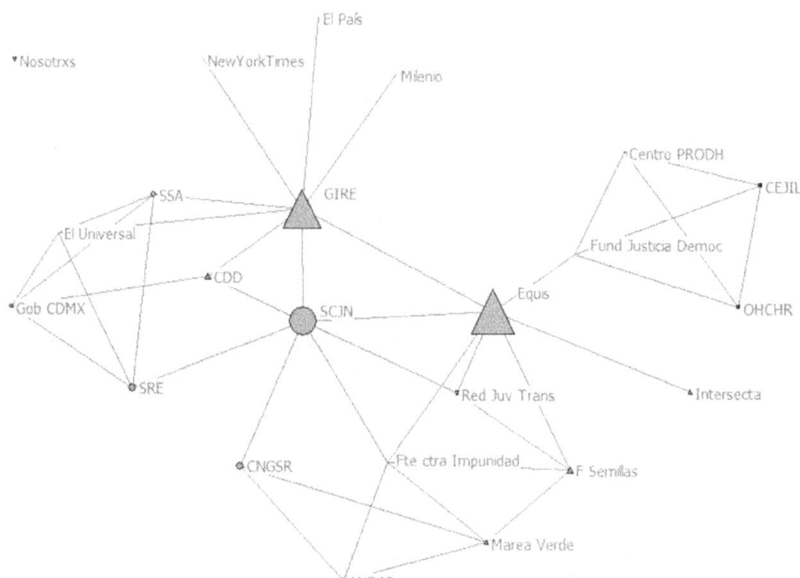

Graph 8 Pro-choice network by betweenness in Mexico (until 2018)
*See Graph 1 for legend

[22] Network analysis was based on name generator questions applied to eight prominent activists of the Mexican pro-choice field.

The betweenness analysis reveals the central position occupied by Equis,[23] GIRE, and the Supreme Court (see Annex). As a professionalized NGO, GIRE led the creation of the Alliance for the Right to Decide (ANDAR) in 2002, which includes organizations such as Catholics for Choice (CDD), Gender Equity, Ipas, and the Population Council. According to Marta Lamas, a recognized feminist who was head of GIRE, this small network was created in response to successive failed efforts to coordinate a large feminist national front on the issue (Lamas, 2015). The network ANDAR, currently comprising only five organizations, is also marked by internal disagreements. In comparison with Brazil, no connecting organization has a central position in the Mexican pro-choice network. In addition, GIRE tried to create three subnational offices (Oaxaca, Sonora, and Veracruz), which was not successsful (I83).

The history of GIRE is particularly interesting in showing that subnetworks in Mexico are specialized in either doctrinal or nondoctrinal issues. It also reveals the key role played by elite contacts in consolidating strategies. This organization was founded by Marta Lamas and Patricia Mercado. The latter was also cofounder of Mujeres en Plural and another organization, Diversa, as well as a candidate for the Mexican presidency. Lamas sees a division of labor between her – dedicated to strategically plan pro-abortion efforts in a very circumscribed territory (Mexico City) – and Patricia, who is involved with political parties and the "realpolitik," that is the everyday politics in Congress. Lamas openly recognizes her social capital as key to GIRE's foundation: "GIRE could be formed because there was social capital, because I knew which doors to knock on, which threads to pull, and whom to call on the phone to help me" (I83). These relationships were central to promoting the pro-choice agenda through top personal contacts in different branches of the national government and Mexico City's government.

These relationships proved to be fruitful, particularly in the centralized Mexico City, where most of the intellectual, cultural, economic, and political elites congregate. The PRD governed the capital from 1988 to 2018. Mexico City was thus one of the first and most important subnational electoral territories to challenge the PRI's long-standing dominance in Mexican politics. After some defeats in Mexico City's Congress in 2003, during Rosario Robles Berlanga's administration, several exceptions on abortion were finally passed in the local legislature. The Alliance and GIRE played a central role by providing information, while Catholics for Choice actively lobbied local catholic deputies.

[23] EQUIS-Justice for Women is a feminist organization that has sought to improve access to justice for women since 2011.

This achievement provoked strong reactions from antiabortion conservatives. The first PAN President, Vicente Fox, mobilized the presidential office to instruct the National Human Rights Commission (CNDH) and the Attorney General's Office to file an action of unconstitutionality in the Supreme Court against the advancements in Mexico City. Feminist pro-choice activists were able to block this effort by contacting allies within the Supreme Court. Their capacity to simultaneously build an enabling network in the local legislature and block conservative reactions in the Supreme Court advanced the pro-choice agenda in Mexico City. In 2006, the network again acted to block conservative antiabortion efforts to stop the application of the Mexican Standard on the Morning After Pill (NOM 046). In this case, the numerous contacts held by the small, elite pro-choice network within the three branches of the federal government prevented conservatives from surreptitiously boycotting the wording of NOM 046.

Within this context, it is not surprising that the Legal Interruption of Pregnancy (ILE) was approved in Mexico City's legislature in 2007. Again, this triumph was the result of intensive political maneuvering within the three branches of both the federal and Mexico City governments – including lobbying both male and female representatives. The enabling network built within the Mexico City executive was particularly striking. It included the mayor himself (Marcelo Ebrard) and involved active and close contact with the legal counselor for the city's government.

The approval of the ILE provoked strong reactions from conservatives, including two appeals of unconstitutionality to the Supreme Court by two states (Baja California and San Luis Potosí). Despite this pressure, in 2008, the Supreme Court confirmed the validity of the law, highlighting once again the effectiveness of the pro-choice network in blocking conservative reactions at the federal level. This led to the implementation of a series of public health measures that would guarantee the ILE in Mexico City (Perez Flores and Amuchastegui Herrera, 2012). However, the approval of this law in the capital triggered antichoice reactions at the subnational level. More than 50 percent of state congresses (twenty out of thirty-two states) passed laws recognizing the right to life from the moment of conception. Thus, advances in one government level generated obstacles in others (Franceschet, 2011).

The next section analyzes the inability of feminist networks in Mexico to block conservative reactions at the subnational level. Returning to our analytical argument, it looks at how efforts to block conservative antiabortion reactions are undermined by the disconnection of the feminist network from (1) intersectional and LGBT+ organizations in the network's horizontal dimension,

(2) political parties over a doctrinal issue in the intermediary dimension, and (3) subnational and marginal populations in the vertical dimension.

3.3 Obstacles to Blocking Conservative Reactions

Abortion exceptions had progressed differently across states up until the approval of the ILE in 2007. Before 1970, most states had approved abortion exceptions for rape cases (Ortiz Ortega, 2019). It was thus not until after the approval of the ILE in 2007 that states, in a visceral reaction, began approving antichoice legislation. As a result, the fetus was given the status of a person protected by the right to life in twenty states, and the criminalization of abortion rose dramatically. Surprisingly, antichoice state constitutional amendments were approved in ten of the fifteen states that had previously adopted progressive abortion exceptions. The backlash was also strikingly fast: only three years after the approval of the ILE, sixteen states passed antichoice local constitutional reforms, increasing to twenty by 2021 (see Beer 2017).[24]

Interestingly, our interviewees expressed surprise at such a reaction at the subnational level. They attributed the success of conservatives across states to the support of the PRI in local legislatures, which is qualified by Lamas as "treason from the woman leader of the PRI at that moment" (I83). The PAN's reaction was expected – being a right-wing party with deep links to the Catholic Church and antiabortion groups. Although the PRI's president at the time, Beatriz Elena Paredes Rangel, was a well-recognized feminist with a close relationship with GIRE, the party was rather focused on winning the next presidential election (2012) – after having lost two previous elections (2000 and 2006) to the right-wing PAN. Electoral considerations in profoundly conservative states thus led the PRI, including its president, to adopt positions in favor of the right to life in several local constitutional amendments.

Considering our argument about network specialization, women politicians involved with "realpolitik" fulfilled their commitments to nondoctrinal issues. It was thus unrealistic to expect unequivocal pro-choice support to supersede electoral considerations for these women. To support a doctrinal issue such as abortion when confronted with high electoral risks would require more extensive, non-elite, intersectional connections among feminists and voters in general. In other words, a high mobilization capacity in favor of abortion at local levels is necessary to reduce the electoral risk of rejection in conservative

[24] States that approved the right to life from conception after the ILE approval in 2007 were: Morelos and Baja California (2008); Colima, Sonora, Quintana Roó, Guanajuato, Durango, Puebla, Nayarit, Jalisco, Yucatán, San Luis Potosí, Oaxaca, and Querétaro (2009); Chiapas and Tamaulipas (2010); Veracruz (2017); Sinaloa (2018); Nuevo León (2019); and Aguascalientes (2021).

electoral territories (see Section 3.4). The pro-choice coalition would have to consolidate a broad, diverse, and intersectional feminist network to achieve this kind of mobilization. It would also have to be geographically dispersed across the subnational territory, which was not the case in Mexico until 2018.

Furthermore, the fact that feminist pro-choice networks did not have the same embeddedness degree among local elites or the population in general as in Mexico City should not be overlooked. Antiabortion groups, in contrast, could rely on the support of the Catholic Church – to which they were linked – as their network intersects with ecclesial parish structures. Also, these groups were strategically connected with economic, political, and social elites at the local level, and with networks of American antiabortion activists (Reuterswärd, 2018). Evidently, the highly specialized, small, elite pro-choice advocacy model implemented in Mexico City could not be easily replicated at the subnational level.

Moreover, vertical coordination with governments was different in each state. Gender-related institutions (women's institutes or secretariats) had achieved distinct levels of consolidation in distinct states. A few women's institutes had existed previously, but the creation of INMUJERES in 2001 triggered the appearance of several new women's institutes – under very different regulatory frameworks – in the thirty-two states of the republic (Tarrés, 2006). Concurrently, some women's institutes at the subnational level were "captured" by religious conservative coalitions, reversing their pro-gender policy orientation and replacing it with one that was pro-family (Zaremberg and Guzmán Lucero, 2019).

Following the backlash at the local level, the main pro-choice organizations of the network turned to the courts. Since 2007, feminists have centered their strategy on litigation through lawsuits (called in Mexico writs of *amparo*) appealing for abortion exceptions based on states' penal codes that exist in parallel with antiabortion amendments. This socio-legal mobilization – developed by GIRE and a new generation of organizations mainly based in Mexico City (e.g. Equis – Justice for Women) – became the main strategy used to overturn discriminatory verdicts. However, writs of amparo do not set a precedent for other cases, on the contrary, they only apply to the individual claimant. Moreover, this legal strategy requires complex, juridical knowledge and consumes a considerable amount of money and time. Groups of disadvantaged women in marginal territories cannot easily resort to socio-legal mobilization. As one of our interviewees clearly stated, the writ of *amparo* in Mexico is "horribly an elite strategy" (I78), an understanding supported by the literature (Pou Giménez, 2014). Finally, judges in local courts are not familiar with the feminist, gender, or even human rights frameworks, and progressive rulings at the national level were slow to reach subnational courts. Consequently, local judges tended to be more conservative in their rulings. In short, the successful strategy implemented in the Supreme Court was not easily replicated in the lower courts. However, this experience provided several pro-choice, feminist institutional activists within the Supreme Court with training in socio-legal mobilization. In 2021, this would pay off (see Section 3.4).

Regarding the subdimension of population (also within the vertical dimension) the disconnect between traditional feminist organizations and intersectional groups is apparently magnified by sectionalized policies that separate the issues of women from those of Indigenous people. As stated by a recognized Indigenous feminist: "the Secretariat for Women [in a state] had another reality and other actions ... we had a good personal relationship, but we never managed to act together ... I felt that they did more programs of what was already established as gender [without including an intersectional perspective" (I84). Afro-Mexican women activists highlighted a similar lack of governmental coordination (I86). These interviewees pointed out that policymaking in Mexico prevents the effective implementation of an intersectional paradigm. The policy process in Brazil, on the other hand, creates opportunities for intersectional network-building. As we will see, in Brazil, contact between black women and classic gender mainstreaming activists was facilitated by the fact that the agenda on women's policy was set through a participatory mechanism (conferences), and also because the horizontal dimension of the Brazilian network is more diversified than that of Mexico; however, that does not prevent conflicts from arising.

On the other hand, regarding the intermediary dimension, the quota laws, approved in local legislatures after 2007, also varied considerably. In 2007, women occupied 10 to 20 percent of legislative seats in fifteen states, 20 to 30 percent in twelve states, and under 10 percent in two states. In only three states did women account for more than 30 percent of the representatives (Zaremberg, 2009). Furthermore, the strength of pro-choice activism in relation to antiabortion activism varied according to the level of influence of the Catholic Church, the strength of the conservative Catholic party, the PAN, and the strength of left-wing parties, specifically the PRD (Beer, 2014; Beer, 2017). As previously mentioned, the PRI played a critical role in tilting the balance toward the approval of antiabortion initiatives at the local level.

Finally, regarding the horizontal dimension, the creation of synergies between pro-choice feminist networks and intersectional feminist organizations at the local level was highly challenging. Inequalities that cut across the movement were repeatedly mentioned by our interviewees. In other words, obstacles to establishing connections within the horizontal dimension of our analytical dimension were particularly hard to overcome. For instance, one of the most remarkable conflicts over abortion involved the Zapatista Women's Movement in Chiapas. Such conflicts arose in the 1990s when the Zapatista Subcomandante Marcos and Marta Lamas publicly discussed the issue in a series of newspaper articles and Zapatista Army communications. While Lamas argued that abortion was a real need for women, including Indigenous women, the Subcommandant replied that "the women comrades say they do not ask for abortion clinics because they do not even have delivery clinics" (Enlace Zapatista, 1994). Considering the important role played by the Zapatista movement within the Indigenous movement in Mexico, it is not surprising that our Indigenous interviewees continue to discuss the complex relationship between their perspectives and those of centralized feminist paradigms (I84).

These obstacles underwent crucial changes between 2019 and 2021. Although this period falls outside our research focus, we have included some transformations to contrast our arguments, given the momentous enabling changes that occurred.

3.4 New Enabling Horizons: Changing Obstacles?

Two developments have recently transformed the pro-abortion scenario in Mexico. These transformations confirm the elite pattern described in the previous section but, at the same time, have opened up a more bottom-up process that has the potential to modify this pattern.

First, in a single month, September 2021, the Supreme Court approved three crucial progressive rulings regarding abortion. On September 7, it approved an action of unconstitutionality (*ação direta de inconstitucionalidade* [ADI]) concerning Coahuila's state constitution. The ADI established the mandatory noncriminalization of abortion throughout the country. Local judges, even conservative ones, could no longer treat abortion as a crime, and there were no exceptions. A few weeks later, the Supreme Court invalidated the provision that protected the right to life from conception, following another ADI related to Sinaloa's state constitution. It was a clear blow to the backlash that had occurred since the approval of the ILE in 2007. Finally, the Supreme Court declared article 10 *bis* of the General Health Law unconstitutional, which related to the conscientious objection of medical and nursing staff. It further called on the federal legislature to establish clear guidelines that would allow such objections without affecting access to abortion services in any way.

An analysis of the political context (particularly the conflicts between the executive and the Supreme Court) that gave rise to these advancements is beyond the scope of this Element. However, we highlight one feature that relates directly to our argument. One respondent pointed out the crucial role played by institutional activists, particularly account clerks and legal advisors, who have developed within a feminist, gendered, and human rights framework: "They are brilliant young lawyers, trained in top universities, very open minded . . . we call them the "secretari*e*s"[in Spanish][25] and it was really them who brilliantly prepared and provided supporting arguments for the rulings" (I78). The same respondent also recognized the importance of gender training programs provided by gender units within the Supreme Court and the Mexican judiciary. Several other interviewees pointed out the network of recognized organizations (GIRE, Equis, ProEquidad, etc.) and their association with the judiciary, which helped provide information and technical juridical knowledge (I91, 92, 94, 81). This confirms our argument regarding the deep embeddedness of a small, elite, pro-choice network within the judiciary.

The second major development, occurring between 2019 and the time the writing of this Element was finished in January 2022, was the approval of pro-abortion bills in four Mexican states: Oaxaca, Hidalgo, Veracruz, and Baja California.[26] These bills were presented by MORENA women deputies and one man. We explored the cases of Oaxaca and Hidalgo, the first and the second states to decriminalize abortion after Mexico City. In these cases, local deputies who were interviewed stressed the importance of the presence of nationally recognized feminists within MORENA, who were able to reduce internal party conflicts within the state fraction composed of both progressive and conservative deputies. In the case of Oaxaca, considered a critical juncture by all interviewees, the personal intermediation by prominent MORENA female politicians at the national level was mentioned as crucial in preventing a potential presidential sanction of the local deputies. Although the president had expressed strongly conservative views regarding abortion and stirred deep conflicts with the feminist movement, he ultimately kept his silence regarding the Oaxacan legislative decision. As one of our interviewees noted: "At the national level [referring to the President], there was no position in favor or against . . . Oaxaca gave a secure sign: this is possible" (I92).

Future research should address parity (and the increase of women deputies at a subnational level), international diffusion, or the party-system transformation as factors that promoted (or not) a substantive pro-abortion agenda in local

[25] The respondent makes reference to the Spanish word "secretarios," the masculine plural form used generically to refer to both male and female. The use of the "e" (instead of "o") is considered inclusive language, denoting adhesion to diversity.

[26] Between the writing and publication of this Element, four further states – Sinaloa, Baja California Sur, Colima, and Guerrero – have decriminalized abortion, making nine states in total (including Mexico City) as of August 2022.

legislatures. A comparison with states where bills were not approved during the same period (such as Puebla or Jalisco) would be needed in order to determine causality. This is beyond the scope of this Element. Nevertheless, it is important to highlight some new features of the pro-choice network evident in recent cases. Drawing on additional exploratory interviews in Oaxaca and Hidalgo, the pro-choice network is illustrated in Graph 9.

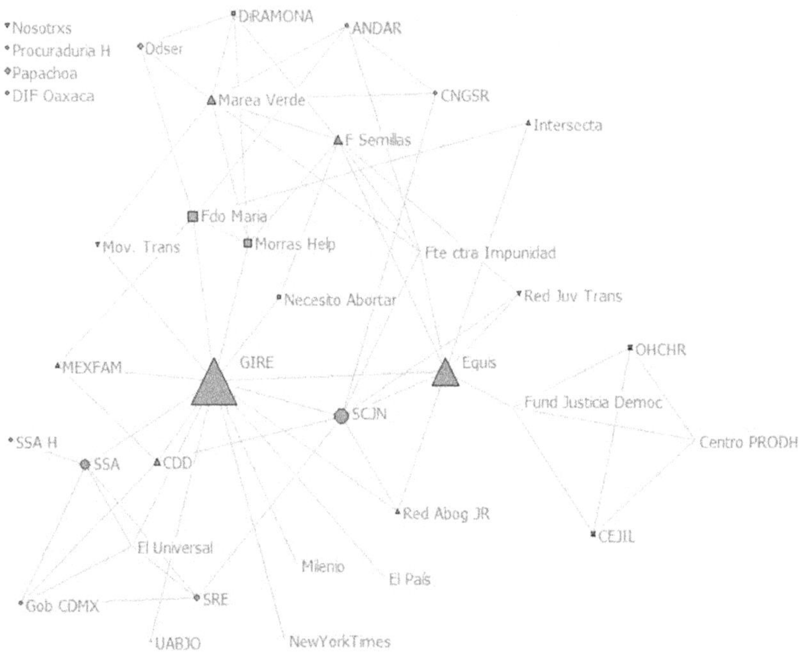

Graph 9 Pro-choice network by betweenness in Mexico (after 2018)
* See Graph 1 for legend

Graph 9 shows that GIRE, Equis, and the Supreme Court continue to occupy central positions within the pro-choice network. However, more importantly, inclusive organizations as Fondo Semillas (Seeds Fund) and Fondo Maria (Maria's Fund) are now also centrally positioned in terms of betweenness, above the mean of this measure (see the Annex). Marea Verde Mexico (Green Tide) is located a few hundredths below the mean, reflecting the impact of international dissemination following the approval of the Voluntary Interruption of Pregnancy (IVE) in Argentina. Fondo Semillas has been supporting other organizations for almost thirty years, within a pluralistic, intersectional, and inclusive framework in terms of sexual identities. Fondo Maria was founded in May 2009 following the approval of the ILE in Mexico City to provide financial, emotional, and logistical support to women from other states who do not have the necessary resources to access the legal abortion services available in the capital city. The graph also shows the fund's connection to both traditional organizations, such as GIRE, and new organizations, particularly collectives such as Morras Help Morras[27] or Necesito Abortar (I Need to Abort), networks of abortion *doulas* (collective that provides support during the abortion process). One organization that works with young Indigenous activists on sexual and reproductive rights at local level, DDSER, also appears in Graph 9. These collectives have a more flexible and innovative organizational structure. Interestingly, this first exploration of the pro-abortion processes in Oaxaca and Hidalgo shows that centrality within the network seems to have shifted to relatively new organizations working in an inclusive and pluralistic manner. In the case of Fondo Semillas, its position appears to reflect a gradual transformation after thirty years of supporting novel and diverse feminist groups, while the cases of the abortion *doulas* collectives and Fondo Maria show the power of a generational, organizational, and leadership transformation within the movement.[28] These developments highlight the novel connections that have been established between classic, centralized organizations (such as GIRE) and relatively new local collectives, political actors, civil society, and governmental organizations.

Interviews with new young leaders of traditional organizations that form part of ANDAR reinforce this notion. This new generation of leaders of classic organizations demonstrates similar characteristics to the institutional activists within the judiciary. They are well trained in juridical litigation, have comprehensive knowledge of the human rights legal framework, both nationally and internationally, and extensive experience in socio-legal mobilization, surprising for their young age. In addition, they are well versed in the framework of women's rights and feminist theory and easily navigate new comunication tools available through social media. This renewal of leadership in old elite organizations appears to have opened up new networks at the local level that are able to take advantage of the current context. In this regard, one interviewee stressed the importance of opportunities presented by the new and flexible online and in-person networking spaces for young, pro-choice activists:

> Before the Pandemic we held these Regional Meetings "Let's talk about abortion," which was a broad call. Whoever wants to come, come! and there was a fairly large network of basically young women ... During the Pandemic these meetings become "Virtual Handkerchiefs." We did a thing

[27] *Morras* is Mexican slang word for young girls with a more popular or street connotation.

[28] Besides the strong ties shown in Graph 9, in Oaxaca, respondents also mentioned the Rosario Castellanos Women's Studies Group A. C. (GESMujer), and in Hidalgo, the State Human Rights Commission (CEDH), UN Women, and local *colectivas* such as the "Feminist Movement of Diverse Women" (MFMD), "Hidalgo Chapter," and "Invictus."

> called "Green Thursdays," which were spaces for conversations about abortion … now we have online fatigue and we have already suspended [these activities], but for sure they will be activated again if necessary. (I94)

The same activist described a general feminist contagion at the local level, referring to not only a renewal of elite organizational leadership (top-down process), but also the flourishing of local organizations (bottom-up proccess). As these two processes intersect, cooperation between classic organizations and the relatively newer network can be observed. This was the case, for example, with the cooperation between GIRE, Morras Help Morras, and other organizations that, in 2020, successfully presented a writ of *amparo* against a conservative bill in Aguascalientes. This cooperation demonstrated how pluralistic cooperation can be effective in blocking conservative attacks.[29]

However, despite promising cooperation, interviewees noted the lingering effects of old obstacles. In both Oaxaca and Hidalgo, deputies and activists stressed the extreme difficulty of managing negotiations and presented a vision of a fragmented and conflictive local feminist movement. As one deputy said:

> Everyone has a position. If one had already reached an agreement to carry out the initiative, then suddenly another group came and they asked for the same thing: "Well, I already talked with those from X" and they say: "Well no, they are from another group, they don't represent us …" and we start again … But, we legislators, are unnecessarily wearing ourselves out, the same organizations among themselves … it does not pay for this [the legislative process] to end, well, faster. (I93)

Interviewees identified two primary conflictive issues that impede cooperation between organizations, and between legislators and organizations. The first is the conflict between institutional and noninstitutional activism:

> That was difficult, to make them [university collectives] understand … because there were people who even today do not accept, do not recognize … and we do not expect them to recognize it, but it is difficult for me to understand what they wanted, what they needed. I opened, knocked on doors, but I could not connect with them … maybe it was hard for me also because I didn't belong to any collective, I came from the institutional part of direct work with women. (I92)

[29] The writ of *amparo* was obtained against the "Pin Parental" bill, which would have granted parents the right to forbid content in educational curricula that they consider to be "gender ideology" (content mainly related to sexual education and LGBT+ rights). The following organizations cooperated for the writ of *amparo*: GIRE, Network for Children's Rights in Mexico (Redim), Being Gay Collective, Terfu A. C., Observatory of Social and Gender Violence, and Morras Help Morras.

The second issue, explained by another interviewee, is the serious conflict between many feminist organizations and transgender organizations in particular, as well as the LGBT+ networks in general:

> I think that this whole issue of the inclusion of Trans people, I would say that right now, it is the issue of conflict between Feminist Movements . . . In the case of Puebla, I find that this was a critical situation. During the Pandemic there was a takeover of the local Congress in Puebla . . . at first, there was great strength or closeness between these movements or feminist people who took over Congress but at the time of the petition, what they were demanding, let's say in the negotiation with the state, that's where all the differences arose [regarding the Trans and LGBT+ agenda]. (I94)

> Trans people support the Feminist Movement . . . you have to acknowledge . . . But the Feminists did not support Trans people, the way Trans people supported the Feminists. (I93)

The gap between some pro-choice feminist organizations and LGBT+ groups is significant and impacts the ability to confront conservative actors. This was particularly evident when the bill to extend LGBT+ rights (e.g. equal marriage) was defeated in the federal legislature in 2018. The lack of coordination between Mexican feminists and LGBT+ activists when facing the National Family Front (associated with antiabortion groups) – which had successfully mobilized across the country – was surprising. As a well-known LGBT+ activist revealed: "The feminist movement is still not sufficiently aware of the strength of conservative actors in Mexico" (I81). Contrary to the Brazilian case, reproductive issues do not appear to be strongly associated with the broader discussion around sexuality in Mexico. As one advocate pointed out:

> In terms of sexuality, Mexico is one of the most backward countries . . . You open any book that says in the title "sexual and reproductive rights" and in the text, you will hardly see a serious discussion on sexual rights. Everything is about reproduction. . . . so [when you do not discuss sexuality] you have the transphobes and I see them closer to the conservative discourse than to the libertarian discourse of the feminist movement. (I81)

Finally, the intersectional connection with Indigenous and Afro women continues to present a challenge for the Mexican pro-choice movement. As another young leader of GIRE commented: "We must move from the vision that indigenous women have the same problems as us because, for example, they have the issue of traditional midwifery, on which they have been working for years and pushing for maternal health issues and the recognition of them as traditional midwives" (I85). In other words, this challenge raises the question of the extent to which feminist activists have been able to connect truly intersectional visions around abortion and sexual and reproductive rights in Mexico.

In sum, the analysis of the Mexican pro-abortion struggle up until 2018 reveals an elite network with privileged access to the three branches of government at the federal level and in the capital, associated with political parties through a nondoctrinal network of women politicians but with weak links to grassroots, Indigenous, and Afro women's movements, as well as the LGBT+ movement. Since 2019, the strength of institutional activism within the judiciary has become evident and new ties have begun to emerge between the centralized organizations and local ones. Meanwhile a renewal of leadership in classic organizations has occurred (top-down) and new, local, young collectives have consolidated (down-up). Promising cases of cooperation in the face of conservative attacks have arisen (as in the case of Aguascalientes), although there is still conflict and distance with regard to sexual identities and even with Indigenous and Afro women networks. This weakness undermines the feminist ability to block conservative antichoice reactions at the subnational level both in terms of their capacity to mobilize against conservatives as well as the ability to strongly negotiate with the state in the event of mobilization (as in Puebla). In Section 4, we examine the Brazilian case and compare it with Mexico.

4 Feminist Networks in Brazil: Blocking Antiabortion Conservatives

The criminalization of abortion practices in Brazil has been regularly challenged by organized feminists in social and state spheres. Although feminist advocacy and activism within the Legislature have been continuous since the 1980s, feminists have mainly accessed the state through the executive branch and participatory institutions. The process that brought them into the state is informed by both their relationship with political institutions during the democratic transition – particularly left-wing parties with strong links to the Catholic Church – and the dissemination of feminist networks across the country. Although this historical process encouraged Brazilian feminists to embrace a broad advocacy agenda that included doctrinal issues such as abortion, unlike in Mexico, women's political institutional presence in the legislature and political parties, and the defense of the quota law, have not necessarily been at the forefront of the feminist struggle. Since 2005, an increasingly conservative presidential coalition has forced the feminist network into a blocking position. Establishing horizontal connections within the movement throughout the territory has been crucial for feminists to resist.

Graph 10 summarizes our arguments on the connections between specific historical processes and the features of the Brazilian nested network:

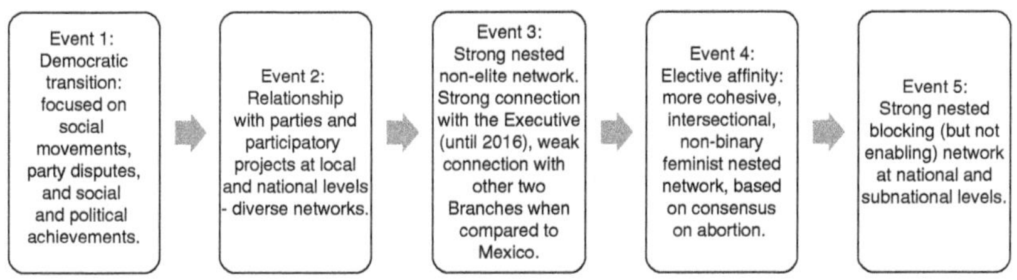

Graph 10 Historical process – Brazil (2003–2018)

4.1 Feminism, Parties, and the State in Brazilian Democratic Transition

Brazilians lived under a military dictatorship from 1964 to 1985, with deleterious consequences for social and political activities. The regime allowed for a single ruling party, the National Renewal Alliance (ARENA), and a single opposition party, the Brazilian Democratic Movement (MDB). The feminist movement did not avoid the abortion issue, nor was it constrained by an interparty consensus as in Mexico. However, its proximity to the Catholic Church and center-left groups and parties (especially the MDB and newly created parties), and its focus on the struggle for democracy, negatively impacted the abortion agenda during the transition (Teles, 1999; Pinto, 2010). Nevertheless, since the 1980s, to advance the agenda on abortion, feminists have organized public demonstrations, attracted media coverage, launched a national campaign, and lobbied representatives in Congress (Barsted, 2009). Moreover, their participation in women's rights councils – created in the states of São Paulo and Minas Gerais – strengthened their relationship with the executive. In 1985, a participatory arena that would later be crucial for organizing the movement's demands within the states and in the Constituent Assembly (1987–88), the National Women's Rights Council (CNDM), was created (Alvarez, 2014).

Advocacy by feminist activists during the constitutional reform – often referred to as the "lipstick lobby" – led to important advancements in labor rights, family planning measures, and maternity and paternity leave policies (I5). The Constituent Assembly also represents the first instance of significant feminist blocking activity, when feminists successfully opposed a proposal to guarantee the right to life from the moment of conception (Barsted, 2009). The fifth article of the 1988 constitution nonetheless protects the right to life, impacting pro-choice activism to this day.

Unlike in Mexico, the Brazilian feminist movement has barely expanded its activism within political parties beyond the left and center-left (Pinto, 2010). Curiously, the Brazilian Women's Letter, which was sent to the Constituent Assembly and contained the ten most prominent issues on the feminist agenda, made no mention of the defense of political rights. Specific issues and strategies have been prioritized based not only on activists' choices but also on constraints on their actions. The Brazilian multiparty system and open-list proportional representation hinder and discourage feminist advocacy within parties, and thus undermine their influence on the electoral system. The existing legislative quota law is ineffective in overcoming underrepresentation – in 2018, only 15 percent of the representatives elected to the National Congress were women – despite the incremental changes proposed since 2009 to compel parties to fulfill the 30 percent quota in their candidate lists, and, more recently, to allocate at least 30 percent of funding to female candidacies. As a result, to overcome women's underrepresentation, activists either propose a comprehensive political reform to move from an open- to a closed-list system with alternation between women and men on the party list (I29, I9), or even defend keeping the existing candidate quota if the proposal is to change to a reserved seats rule in the legislature with a lower percentage than the current 30 percent of candidacies (I7).

Moreover, feminists connected with the nascent PT and its defense of a democratic-participatory project that emphasized participation as the reorganizing principle of the relationship between state and society (Dagnino, 2004). Brazilian democratization was not a return to old parties banished from the political system (or pushed aside by the lack of free competition, as in Mexico), but rather, the creation of new parties committed to democracy and eager to increase the plurality of the system. In addition, participation was channeled into the political system with the creation of collegiate bodies – such as councils and conferences – comprising governmental and social actors. Thus, while a new representative government was being built, movements demanded participation, rather than representation, to oppose authoritarianism.

After resigning from the CNDM in 1990,[30] feminists participated mainly through women's rights and healthcare councils. The synergy between feminists and the *sanitarista* movement[31] – coupled with the dual militancy of activists in both movements – significantly impacted the women's health agenda (Dehesa, 2019). By occupying positions within the Ministry of Health and participating in the National Health Council and thematic conferences,

[30] This resignation resulted from the withdrawal of the council's financial and administrative autonomy, after the election of President Fernando Collor.

[31] This movement was made up of middle-class health professionals calling for widespread, equitable access to medical care and preventive health services in Brazil.

feminists built a strong relationship with the *sanitarista* movement throughout the 1990s. The feminist movement developed from the internationally financed NGOs that were spreading in that decade and were subsequently incorporated into the state – mainly into the executive – as providers of social services (Alvarez, 2014; Medeiros and Fanti, 2017). Participation in policy-making processes occurred at the state and municipal levels, particularly under the PT administration.

In addition to maintaining a relationship with legislators who favored broadening abortion rights, feminists tried to influence the creation of a network of public health services to guarantee legal abortion exceptions.[32] With respect to the judicial branch, feminists accessed it mostly at the local level, either with requests for abortion in nonlegalized cases of serious fetal anomaly or attempts to guarantee public access to abortion services in cases of legal exceptions (Fanti, 2017).

4.2 Network on Reproductive Rights: The Feminists' Enabling Phase

After Lula da Silva won the presidential election with the PT in 2002, union leaders, social movements, and feminists began occupying high- and mid-level positions in the federal government. The president's first goodwill gesture to the feminists was the creation, in 2003, of the Special Secretariat for Women's Policies (SPM), whose ranks were filled with experienced gender activists. In line with this participatory project, the relationship between feminists and the CNDM was re-established. The number of social movement representatives increased, they began to be chosen by their peers through elections, and women's councils spread across the country, reaching 15 percent of all municipalities (Almeida, 2020; Gutterres, Vianna and Aguião, 2014).[33] The capacity to reach marginal populations (vertical dimension) also improved during the PT administrations, with an increase in public agencies for women from 13 in 2004 to 795 in 2016 across the twenty-six states and the federal district (SPM, 2016). Furthermore, the first National Women's Rights Conference was held in 2004, followed by three more in 2007, 2011, and 2016. These conferences were institutional mechanisms aimed at shaping policy agendas in collaboration with citizens, bringing together a large number of participants – between 2,000 and 3,000 nationally – from municipal, state, and national levels.

[32] Since 1940, according to the Penal Code, exceptions refer to cases of rape or danger to the woman's life. The law does not guarantee access to public services, since few hospitals provide this service and doctors can refuse to practice abortion.

[33] This is a very small number when compared with social policy councils that reach the entire country, such as health care; however, it is still more widespread than in Mexico.

The CNDM was responsible for formulating the National Plan of Public Policies for Women and monitored its implementation based on the conference guidelines.

National conferences were key moments for the nesting of the various feminisms in both the horizontal and vertical dimensions. While a qualitative analysis of the conferences reveals that black women, the indigenous movement, and young and nonbinary organizations did not participate on an equal footing with traditional gender organizations (Matos and Alvarez, 2018), conferences did allow the state to reach marginal populations in different parts of the country and include their demands into the decision-making process, as well as contributing to the diversification of the nested network. In particular, the Black Women's Movement increased its participation in the conferences and improved its coordination with feminist movements. This plurality generated relevant discussions and proposals on abortion, giving pro-choice activists a direction (Martello, 2018).

While in Mexico we identified a long-lasting, circumscribed, specialized network on reproductive rights, in Brazil that was not the case. Due to the movements' broad agenda on women's rights, which includes issues such as violence, reproductive rights, racism, patriarchy, political rights, and so on, pro-choice activism is dispersed across several organizations. As an activist has said when asked to locate her own organization within one of three categories (binary, LGBT+, or intersectional), "it is a feminist organization that deals with any feminist issue." She also saw feminism in Brazil as "very mixed . . . . So, you can say that the Articulation of Brazilian Black Women defends black feminism, great, but . . . there are several elements other than just black feminism" (I29).

The Brazilian Articulation for the Right to Safe and Legal Abortion (Jornadas),[34] created in 2004, was a short-lived network composed of feminist activists, feminist organizations, rural workers associations, and midwives from nearly all Brazilian states (Barsted, 2009: 247). Jornadas pushed for bills to expand the scope of legal abortion, and, in cooperation with institutional activists within the CNDM and SPM, it built an active network during Lula da Silva's first term and approved a proposal for legalizing abortion in the first national conference.

Graph 11 presents an abortion network built based on eleven interviews, in which respondents were asked about the issue regarding the 2003–20 period.[35]

The presence of nodes of different shapes indicates a diverse abortion network. It also attests to the importance of connecting organizations. The network includes

[34] This is short for Jornadas Brasileiras pelo Direito ao Aborto Legal e Seguro.

[35] Although the time frame of this study is from 2003 to 2018, most of the interviews were conducted between 2019 and 2020.

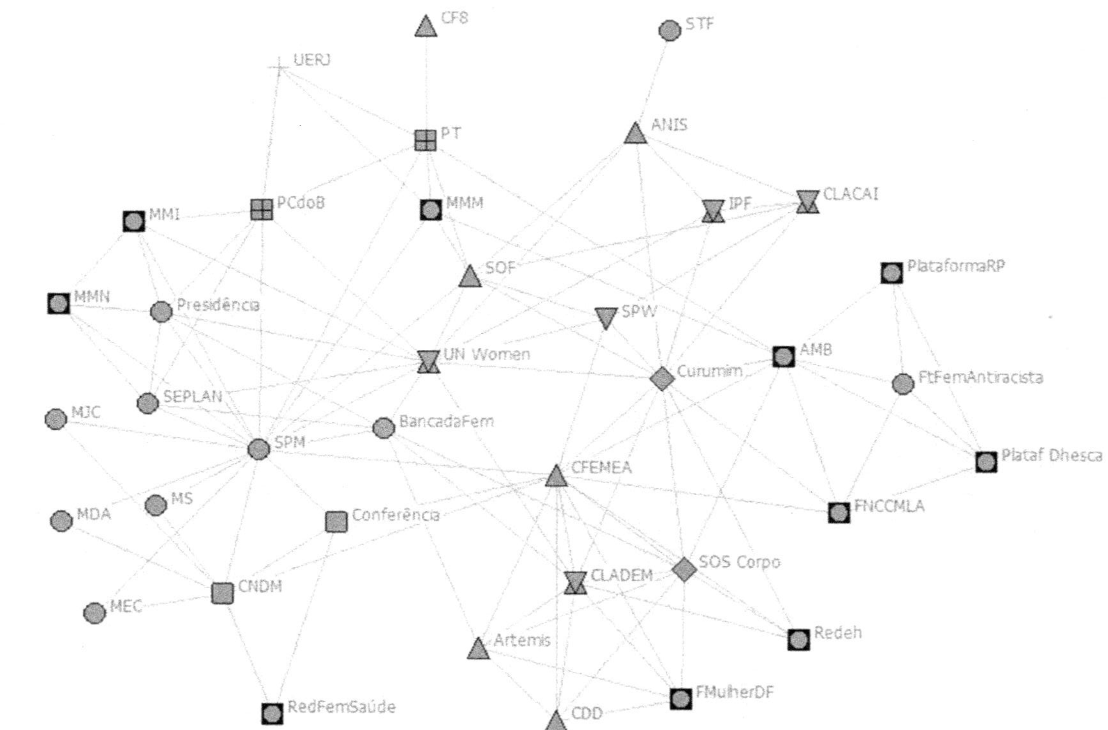

Graph 11 Abortion network (2003–2020)

* See Graph 1 for legend

organizations acting on classic gender and intersectional issues, international networks, executive bodies and legislative fronts, participatory arenas, and political parties. The strong presence of left-wing parties and executive bodies confirms our first impression of relatively weak vertical coordination with the legislative and judiciary in comparison with Mexico.

Graph 12 shows the central position occupied by the SPM in terms of betweenness until the 2016 impeachment – and, consequently, by the CNDM, given its direct connection to the SPM. The CFEMEA, a feminist advocacy NGO focusing on the legislature since 1989, takes the second central position. The AMB, PT, and Curumim Group (an intersectional organization in the state of Pernambuco) also take central roles during this period.

The relationship between feminists, the executive branch, and left-wing parties has provided relational, material, and institutional resources to advance the reproductive rights agenda. In line with the first national conference deliberation, feminists drafted a preliminary pro-choice bill. This bill was assessed by a tripartite legislative committee comprising members of the executive, legislature, and civil society organizations – including two representatives of Jornadas.Although this committee was created with the support of the newly inaugurated PT administration, it was not free of tensions. The increasing influence of evangelical, catholic, and conservative actors in the governmental coalition, coupled with corruption accusations – known as the *Mensalão* Scandal[36] – a few days before the committee's inauguration, led President Lula da Silva to withdraw his support to the abortion agenda. One activist said: "She [Nilceia Freire, the SPM Minister] arrived at the last minute in Congress to present the bill, shaking. We sang the national anthem while the friars were performing an exorcism inside the room. With crosses. Quite symbolic" (I14). Feminists participated actively in the Committee, but then "the government washed their hands" (I30). The election of a conservative as president of the National Congress and the lack of presidential support eventually led the bill to be rejected by the committee in 2008.

Attempts to expand abortion rights in the legislative persisted but declined notably in Lula's second term. While twenty pro-choice bills were introduced during the 2003–6 legislature, only two were presented in the following legislature (Luna, 2014). The III Human Rights National Plan (2009) was an important initiative formulated by different civil society organizations and social movements throughout the country. Although the plan initially recommended that the

[36] *Mensalão* was a corruption scheme that used public funds to pay coalition parties for political support.

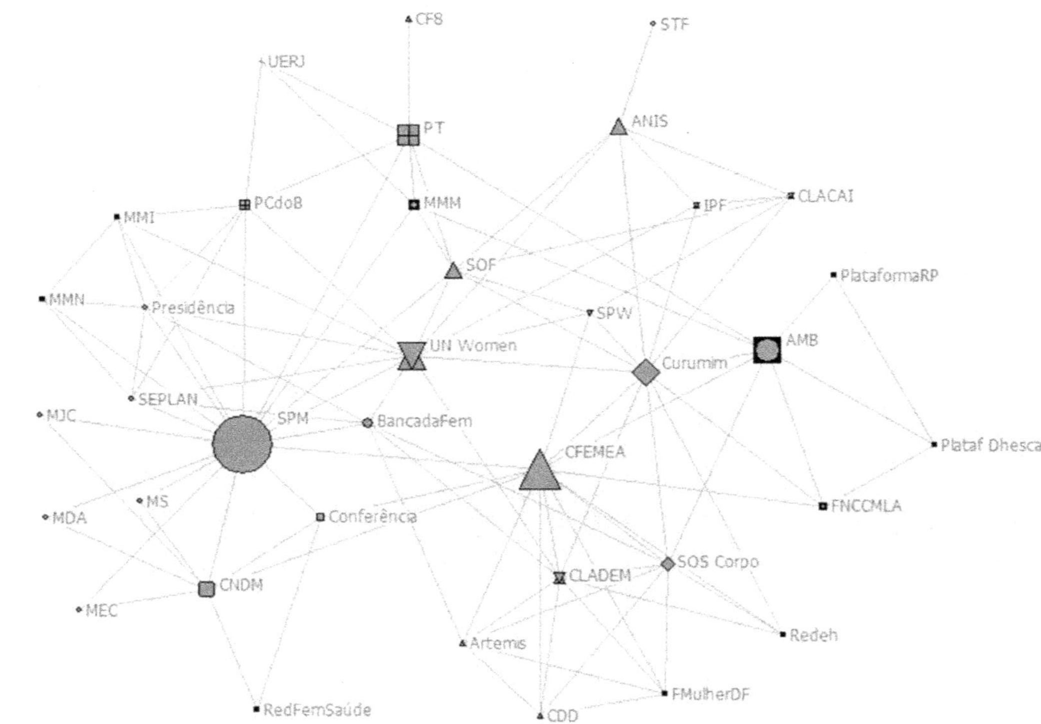

Graph 12 Abortion network by betweenness before the 2016 impeachment

* See Graph 1 for legend

abortion issue be addressed (in terms of women's autonomy) by the legislature, this recommendation was later withdrawn from it (Mariano and Biroli, 2012; Lacerda, 2018).

Nevertheless, in the executive, the SPM and its connection with other ministries yielded more positive results, albeit in a contentious fashion. The implementation of technical regulations and national programs facilitated women's access to family planning, health care in childbirth, contraceptive supply, sterilization surgery, humanized birth, and public assistance for legal abortion. The revision of the technical regulations establishing guidelines for legal abortion exceptions, and the defense of abortion as a public health issue by two health ministers – Humberto Costa in 2005 and José Gomes Temporão in 2007 – contributed to improving the provision of health services across the country. Abers (2020) also provides illustrative examples of institutional activists' efforts to regulate the use of instant pregnancy tests – employed in the public system since 2013 – and to design the protocols for healthcare professionals dealing with cases of unwanted pregnancy.

Compared to Mexico, the relationship with the judiciary was not as crucial for feminists in Brazil during the 2003–18 period. Nevertheless, interviewees mentioned their connections with public defenders' offices in the states, the Public Prosecution Office, feminist public prosecutors, judges, and the Popular Lawyers National Network (RENAP) (I23, 30, 6, 4). They raised serious questions about the adequacy of the strategies used by feminists in the judiciary, particularly given the ambiguous political position of the Supreme Court (STF): "The Judiciary legitimizes the most harmful policies in Brazil recently. Luís Roberto Barroso [one of the STF justices], who has dark attitudes about Brazil and the economy, is the same minister who makes a beautiful vote on LGBT marriage" (I23). Furthermore, feminists stress the risks of imposing legal decisions without societal support (I6). They also fear that losing in the STF would create an insurmountable barrier to advancing abortion rights in the legislature.

Despite these controversies, there has been strategic litigation in the STF, led especially by the NGO ANIS, which is responsible for connecting the abortion network with this court (see Graph 11). The first legal case, Statement of Non-Compliance with Fundamental Precept N. 54 (ADPF), was brought by the National Confederation of Health Workers[37] with the support of ANIS, arguing that terminating a pregnancy of an anencephalic fetus should not be considered

[37] The organization ANIS allied itself with this confederation to circumvent the impossibility of presenting a motion to the court. According to the Brazilian Constitution, nine institutional actors can directly challenge the constitutionality of a law in the Supreme Court, among them political parties and national, class, or union confederations.

a crime. Other feminist organizations participated through STF's societal channels of participation, such as *amicus curae* and public hearings (nonexistent in the Mexican judiciary) to defend the ADPF. The NGO Citizenship, Study, Research, Information, and Action (CEPIA), in association with the CNDM, launched a public campaign supporting the ADPF (Fanti, 2017). After some conservative ADIs were filed, and a long road of judicial advocacy was taken, the STF, in 2012, finally recognized fetal anencephaly as the third exception for legal abortions in the country. This decision followed seven unsuccessful bills that had been introduced between 1992 and 2007 in Congress (Biroli, 2016).

4.3 The Conservative Backlash: Turning into a Blocking Network

The reaction triggered by the enabling network is still seen in the state and public sphere. Four conservative parliamentary fronts were organized since 2005, and antiabortion discourse increased after 2007 in reaction to the feminist's mobilization in the executive, legislative, and judicial branches (Miguel, Biroli, and Mariano, 2017). In addition, the antiabortion movement, which dates back to the 1990s, moved from a defensive to an offensive strategy in 2007 (Rocha, 2020). In contrast to the religious fundaments previously mobilized, conservatives are increasingly using secular arguments in and out of Congress, attesting to their capacity to efficiently frame political disputes and incorporate different adherents to their cause, including parties across practically the entire ideological spectrum. Conservatives saw the 2010 electoral cycle as a political opportunity, and abortion dominated the debate. The growing electoral dependence of the PT on conservative parties resulted in a strategic retreat from this agenda. Feminist activists moderated their discourse, avoiding using the word "abortion," while also trying to pragmatically advance other causes, such as violence, within the SPM (I11).

As of the 2007–10 legislature, all previous progress began to go into reverse. The number of evangelicals in Congress increased dramatically, from fifty-nine in 2003 to sixty-three in 2010, seventy-three in 2014, and eighty-four in 2018. In addition to the defeats, both the Ministry of Health's technical regulation regarding abortion, and Executive Order N. 415 – which had increased doctors' remuneration for legal abortion in the public health system – were revoked, and a new order (N. 1.508/2005) hindering access to legal abortion was instituted.

While during the 2003–6 legislature, seventeen antiabortion bills were introduced, in 2007–10 the number rose to thirty-four, followed by twenty-seven bills in the next legislature (2011–14).[38] Among them, the following are

[38] Analysis conducted by Anne Karoline Rodrigues Vieira for her doctoral thesis in progress at the University of Brasilia, based on the information systems of the House of Representatives and the Federal Senate.

particularly noteworthy: Bill 7.443/2006, which categorizes abortion as a heinous crime; the "Unborn Statute" (Bill 478/2007), which guarantees integral protection to the unborn; the Constitutional Amendment Proposal (PEC) 164/2012, which protects life from conception; the Family Statute Bill (Bill 6.583/2013); Bill 5.069/2013, requiring the presentation of a police report to access abortion services in cases of rape; and the PEC 29/2015 regarding the inviolability of the right to life from conception (Luna, 2014; Miguel, Biroli, and Mariano, 2017). Some of these legislative proposals have not yet been voted on, while others have already been approved or rejected in a legislative committee. Conservatives have also focused on sexual rights, with a growing campaign to negate the term "gender," condemn "homosexuality," and oppose pro-LGBT+ bills, all of which have reinforced the conservative mood in the Chamber of Deputies (Lacerda, 2018). A further complicating factor was Eduardo Cunha's presidency in the Federal Chamber between 2015 and 2016, when he formed a coalition composed of legislators from thirteen right and far-right parties of the *Centrão* (220 deputies or 43 percent of the chamber). Although Cunha was affiliated with the MDB, which was part of the presidential coalition, he initiated the impeachment process. During the 2016 impeachment trial, considered illegimate by feminists, and after Vice President Michel Temer took over as Brazil's interim president, changing the political orientation of the governing coalition, feminists resigned from the CNDM, concluding that, once again, no advancements would be made in this arena.

The backlash was in progress while conservatives' political advantage in Congress was high, the president's party coalition was eroded, and public opposition to abortion rights was increasing. So why was an antiabortion bill not approved? How were feminists able to oppose conservatives?

To answer these questions, we highlight the feminists' capacity to turn itself into a blocking network. Three conditions affected the formation of this network: the characteristics of the Brazilian political system; the intermediary role of political parties, and the horizontal dimension of the feminist network. First, there are certain institutional arrangements in Brazil constraining dramatic changes in legislation. The Brazilian Constitution assigns jurisdiction over the right to life to the federal level, which complicates feminist efforts to build a broad enabling network and support abortion rights since federal legislators must answer to local elites – generally opposed to abortion (Franceschet, 2011). However, the fragmented multiparty National Congress hinders the passing of controversial bills from both progressives and conservatives. In 2018, representatives of thirty different parties were elected to Congress, creating a wide array of political inclinations regarding abortion, many of which do not support radical bills suppressing rights (Miguel, Biroli and Mariano, 2017).

Moreover, the legislative process involves several stages, and the president of the chamber has the power to determine which bills are included in the agenda and which will be put to a vote.

Second, political parties tend to not only prioritize less controversial issues but also abstain from conflict by not openly criminalizing abortion at the federal level, as was the case of the PT and other center-right parties. As pointed out by one interviewee, the executive, after the tripartite committee, declared that "it wasn't going to be against abortion, but it wasn't going to be for it either" (I18). Third, according to Hochstetler (2011), although innovation is always a possibility, blocking coalitions are most likely to emerge when they can be built from existing experiences and networks of mobilization. This includes state and social networks, since activism within the state can be most effective when supported by extra-state network resources (Abers, 2020). In our case, while previous links with the state and participatory institutions were crucial, the Brazilian feminist network was only weakly connected to the different branches of government, particularly considering its poor representation in the legislature and scant cross-party representation, resulting from the ineffectiveness of the quota system. The crisis in the PT's coalition may have led to greater conservative power to push through their policies if only the vertical subdimension of the network was considered. However, the network's capacity to expand its reach across the country, as well as to respond to the demands of marginalized sectors of the society, and connect with distinct social movements, was crucial to blocking conservatives.

These links with society are seen in the National Front against the Criminalization of Women and for the Legalization of Abortion (FNCCLA), created in 2008. This network had more ambitious plans than Jornadas, summarized in two goals: "First, it seeks a broad connection with movements and policy areas beyond the feminist field. Second, it sees winning support in society as a strategy" (I29). Thus, it emphasized the importance of changing public opinion on abortion, framing it as an issue of women's health and reproductive justice – an argument that resonates with black women's demands. The FNCCLA is as important for feminism in Brazil as Mujeres en Plural is in Mexico; however, the former defends a doctrinal issue and has a more diversified horizontal dimension.

The FNCCLA benefited from the existence of a well-connected feminist network working in Congress and the executive. Such network has built alliances with the SPM and certain congresswomen and men and has the support of CFEMEA, which monitors the bills introduced in Congress. In 2020 alone, out of the sixty-two bills regarding reproductive and sexual rights, twenty-seven were antiabortion, and nineteen represented a reaction to governmental measures against abortion rights. Another arena for feminists to coordinate in Congress was the office of the Special Advocate for Women (*Procuradoria da Mulher*), created in 2009 to facilitate political coordination, policy monitoring, information dissemination, and assistance in drafting bills regarding women's rights. Finally, there was the Feminine Parliamentary Group in Congress (composed of all the women deputies and senators) – although only a minority of their members supports abortion rights.

Given that Congress came to be the prime arena for conservative attacks, feminists have engaged in disputing policy content. For that, they leverage their network resources and use various blocking strategies based on their knowledge of the legislative processes. The PT continued to play an intermediary role. Institutional activists in the SPM and other ministries (e.g. health and agrarian development), as well as feminists' members of the PT, pressured the executive to urge party leaders to block conservative proposals, and to discipline deputies within the PT itself: "I once alerted a church deputy: with your political base, you do as you want, [but] in Congress you don't talk about [against] abortion anymore, if you do, I'll file an ethical case against you in the party" (I12).

Feminist activists sometimes acted to prevent antichoice debates in Congress. In 2008, when conservatives attempted to install a Parliamentary Committee of Investigation to probe into clandestine abortions, activists used their influence within the party to delay it by pressuring the president of the Federal Chamber, at the time a PT congressman. "We stayed for one week in the Chamber. ... Arlindo Chinaglia (the president) did not include the topic in the agenda. We met with him for one hour and we managed to convince him." After convincing the president, the feminists successfully lobbied deputies to remove their signatures supporting the committee's creation (I11).

They also attempted to delay or change legislative proposals. This strategy involved disputing both the selection of the committees' rapporteurs and the bills' content. Whenever a bill was sent to a committee, feminists pressured deputies into introducing several amendments: "[in] a bill that has five or three articles, our legislators create a hundred amendments ... if we can't handle it, at least we change something" (I11). Strategies to prevent a vote were also used: "Many times, we asked the leader to go on the attack, to fight, to delay voting, or the government ordered everyone to leave the plenary, so they did not form a quorum to vote" (I11). Feminists' physical presence during plenary sections was crucial to the negotiations, which sometimes involved the minister of the SPM and feminist leaders.

With Eduardo Cunha as president of the Federal Chamber, the political environment changed for the worse. In order to ensure a continuing blocking network, feminists changed strategies: they moved beyond Congress and connected with movements and organizations across the country. The cycle of protests initiated in June 2013 in Brazil is recognized as a feminist revival embracing new generations of activists who took to the streets and social media platforms (Bogado, 2018). Although these diverse groups have criticized feminist mainstreaming within the state and defended horizontal forms of organization, they have nested together against the conservative backlash in the country. Large-scale demonstrations were held in 2015, such as the Daisy March by rural women workers. In November that same year, a series of protests – known as the Feminist Spring – brought millions of women onto the streets in many cities objecting to Bill 5.069/2013 and demanding "Cunha Out!" (I22). A few days later, the first Black Women's National March was organized in Brasilia, bringing together different groups of people and various expressions of feminism (Bogado, 2018). Feminists also denounced Eduardo Cunha and twelve federal deputies to the Organization of American States.

Bill 5.069/2013, introduced by Cunha and signed by twelve other evangelical and catholic deputies, was approved by the Committee of Constitution, Justice, and Citizenship; however, at the beginning of 2022, it had still not been put to a vote in the plenary. In 2016, the impeachment process took center stage in Congress, and Eduardo Cunha was forced to withdraw from the presidency after facing allegations of corruption. His mandate was revoked, and he was subsequently arrested in "Operation Car Wash."[39]

The 2016 impeachment trial and the subsequent removal of Dilma Rousseff from the presidential office rapidly affected the connections between feminists and the state. As shown in Graph 13, the CNDM and SPM lost their roles as intermediaries as the main movements resigned from the CNDM and the new government made changes to the SPM. The AMB (represented by a circle in a box) in particular took up the primary structural position in terms of betweenness, demonstrating once again its importance. The AMB is followed by CFEMEA and Curumim. The FNCCLA, the PSOL, and the Antiracist Feminist Parliamentary Front (FtFemAntirracista) only appeared in the network after 2016.

During this period of political polarization, feminists not only mobilized on the streets and social media platforms but also moved closer to the STF. In 2016, ANIS, in partnership with the National Association of Public Defenders, presented ADI 5.581, requesting permission for abortion in cases of microcephaly associated with the Zika virus. Feminist organizations acted as *amicus curae* in

[39] Operation "Car Wash" was a corruption investigation led by the Federal Police in Brazil. The corruption scheme involved officials of the state-owned oil company Petrobrás, and politicians from several political parties.

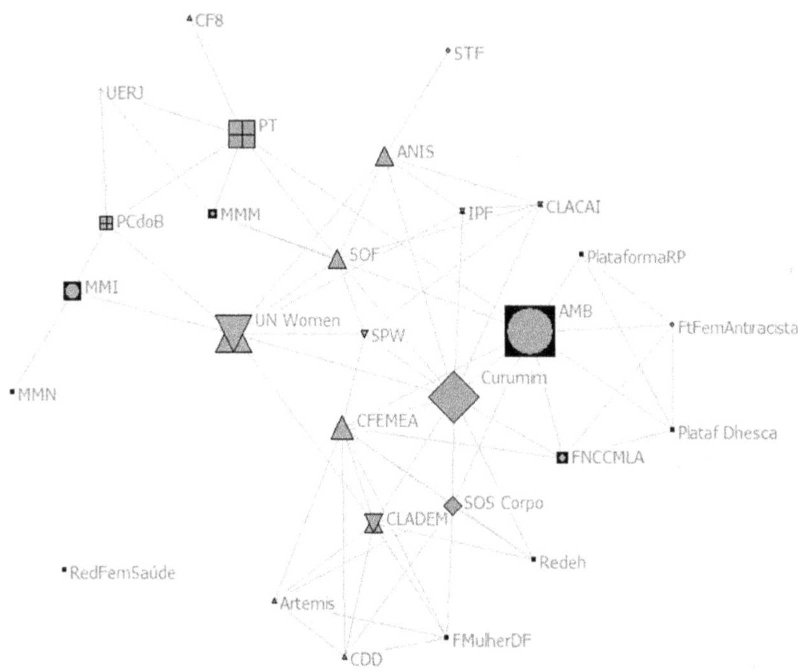

Graph 13 Abortion network after the 2016 impeachment by betweenness
* See Graph 1 for shape code

the process. This ADI, however, was rejected by the STF in May 2020. According to Sorj (2018), in 2016, she and other feminists presented the president of the STF with a petition for the decriminalization of abortion. Additionally, the PSOL – with the support of ANIS but without previous agreement with the feminist movement – presented ADPF 442 proposing to decriminalize abortion during the first twelve weeks of pregnancy, which is still to be voted on.

This legal action created tensions between feminists and ANIS: "That was not an agreement within Brazilian feminism. We have a national front that brings together many women. And judicialization is not a strategy agreed on with the entities" (I6). Furthermore, conflict arose over the content of the ADPF that called for decriminalization of women rather than legalization of abortion. Despite these disagreements, confirmed in various interviews (I6, 13, 14, 23, 31), the movement took advantage of the debate and publicized the issue. Feminist networks attended a public hearing in the STF in 2018 to discuss and support ADPF 442 (Alvarez, 2019). A large "Festival for Women's Lives" was held outside the STF building, uniting heterogeneous coalitions of feminist activists, such as NGOs, party activists, black and Indigenous movements, *quilombolas*, trans and nonbinary people, lesbians, young people, and rural workers. According to an interviewee, "We knew the judiciary was not going to approve it. But we connected with lawyers, jurists, communicators, sociologists, feminists, and NGOs when preparing the feminist action in the public hearing. Everyone was connected, one complementing the other, meeting with those who would talk in the public hearings to make sure the same argument was not repeated, a strategy very well done" (I14). The horizontal dimension was once again activated in a display of feminist unity in defense of abortion rights.

Since Dilma Rousseff's impeachment, the conservative attacks in Congress have remained intense: thirty-one antiabortion bills were introduced between 2015 and 2018. With Bolsonaro's election in 2018, in a period of just three years (2019–2021), forty-five bills have been introduced on this issue. In addition, conservative attacks started coming directly from the executive, and strategic litigation has emerged as an alternative, particularly given the difficulties in mobilizing during the Covid-19 pandemic. The CFEMEA and other organizations are still monitoring bills in Congress, and lobbying deputies with messages. However, Bolsonaro's administration has constrained feminists' blocking activities. Through decrees and executive orders, the federal government has restricted access to reproductive rights, hindering the implementation of legal abortion exceptions, reducing the number of hospitals capable of performing abortions, and intimidating health professionals and women, who are required to present police reports in cases of rape, and ultrasound images of the embryo before the procedure (Executive Order No. 2282/2020). This order drew heavy criticism and prompted five center-left political parties to bring the case to the STF (ADPF 737). Congressional representatives have also issued legislative decrees in an attempt to revoke this policy and submitted information requests for the executive to explain the order, which still requests police reports.

In sum, nested feminist networks' ability to confront conservatives is possibly a matter of perspective. While feminists in Brazil had less institutional access to the three branches of government compared to Mexico, the Brazilian network displayed greater plurality and presence throughout the country than its Mexican counterpart. In a moment of backlash, this relational resource was crucial to blocking conservatives at the national level. It is unknown whether a strong conservative backlash has led feminism to be more diverse and well connected in Brazil. Moreover, this diversity is rooted in a history of political mobilization at the local and national level during the democratic transition. The nested feminist network in Brazil, unlike the one in Mexico, did not put much effort into advancing women's political rights in the legislative branch – not even within left-wing political parties. This neglect – along with different institutional and contextual factors – affected its pro-choice enabling strategy. All the same, for almost two decades, Brazilian feminists have been extremely efficient in mobilizing their horizontal connections to block antiabortion reactions – a capacity that is currently being threatened.

5 Conclusions and Directions for Future Research

Feminist struggles for gender equality and progressive policy change regarding women's rights have triggered conservative responses around the world. In this Element, we have argued that feminists' ability to successfully counter the conservative backlash is impacted by the complex dynamics within the feminist field as well as between feminism and the state. To account for this complexity, we proposed the concept of nested feminist networks. Nested networks are oriented toward enabling particular policy outcomes and blocking conservative reactions. They comprise three dimensions in relation to the movement's plurality across intersectional and sexual identity issues (horizontal), its relationship with the multifaceted state, including its branches, territory, and population (vertical), and the mediating role of political institutions in this relationship (intermediary).

By comparing the Brazilian and Mexican nested feminist networks until 2018 (with some highlights after this period), three main lessons have been learned. First, contrary to the claim that plurality weakens feminism by undermining its main political subject (women), our analysis suggests that feminism is rather strengthened by its ability to nest together with intersectional and LGBT+ organizations when confronting conservative reactions. The Brazilian case – with feminists facing a huge conservative backlash since 2007 – substantiates this argument. The horizontal – albeit conflictive – coordination within the movement and with multiple organizations, including those of black women and LGBT+ activists at the national and subnational levels, has contributed to the construction of a long-standing blocking coalition that has increased feminists' resistance within the legislative branch and on the streets. Connecting organizations (such as the AMB and the FNCCLA) and participatory processes have also played a key role in creating a more coordinated and plural network. The historical imprint of the democratic transition – with social movements and center-left parties as allies – enabled a doctrinal feminist agenda on abortion, and included a wide range of feminism(s). Further research should explore the potential endogeneity concerning a causal relationship between better coordination between a heterogeneous feminism and a more intense conservative backlash in the country.

In contrast, a small, professionalized Mexican pro-choice network, strongly associated with elite actors throughout the three branches of government, was not able to deal with conservative reactions at the local level until 2018. Lack of connections with intersectional feminists and LGBT+ activists limited the scope of this network. As local elites are affiliated with Catholic and religious groups, including antiabortion organizations, the strategy to leverage abortion from above, as in the case of Mexico City, was not successful at the subnational level. Exploratory information after 2018 shows that novel connections between classic and new organizations at the local level created a more favorable context in which to promote pro-choice bills or face conservative attacks.

This result suggests that we should address the disputes created around gender binarism versus queer or intersectional theories and activism from another point of view. We do not attempt to resolve these discussions. They imply delicate theoretical and pragmatic issues that demand more in-depth analysis, which exceeds the scope of this Element. However, from a sociopolitical, relational point of view, our findings show that the feminist struggle against the conservative backlash is strengthened – rather than undermined – by greater plurality and coordination.

The second lesson points to the importance of political access to the state. By disdaining battles within state institutions, activists pay a high price in terms of both enabling and blocking results. Mexican feminists have built a strong, nondoctrinal interparty consensus that has increasingly given them influence in Congress, while their Brazilian counterparts remained weak in this regard. In Mexico, this consensus did not help blocking conservative reactions at the local level where it entailed electoral costs for women politicians, but it was valuable in ensuring the extensive presence of feminist activists within the legislative, judicial, and executive branches at the federal level. Until 2018, this presence contributed to blocking conservative attacks at the national level and to tabling an abortion bill in Mexico City. After 2018, the embeddedness within the judiciary branch allowed historical pro-choice enabling rulings. In contrast, Brazilian feminist activism increased incrementally within the executive (including the set of participatory institutions) and left-wing parties, with continuous advocacy practices in the legislature, which allowed them to block legislative proposals but not build an enabling coalition around this doctrinal issue. Pro-choice legal mobilization related to the judiciary was not entirely absent, but it still causes considerable controversy within the movement.

Third, consistent with the arguments of McBride Stetson (2001) and Htun and Weldon (2018), we found that close ties with left-wing programmatic parties are important, but not sufficient, to advance the pro-choice agenda (as attested by the case of the pro-abortion bill in Brazil, defeated in 2008).

Certainly, should the left-wing parties abandon the defense of abortion (i.e. if they embrace a conservative agenda), this proposition becomes problematic.[40] Our findings nevertheless offer an additional, more nuanced layer of understanding. They suggest that political parties have a key role to play as intermediaries between feminist movements and the state, albeit with paradoxical interchanges between enabling and blocking results. On the one hand, the defeat of pro-choice initiatives in Brazil exposes the fragility of a relationship built exclusively with center-left parties for advancing a controversial doctrinal issue – although the same alliance provided political and institutional resources to block conservative reactions. On the other hand, the presence of Mexican women politicians across parties from practically the entire ideological spectrum was crucial for advancing political rights and obstructing conservatives at the national level but ineffective at blocking them and expanding abortion rights at the local level. In other words, blocking antiabortion reactions without a close alliance with a programmatic left-wing party seems unlikely. However, it is equally improbable to advance pro-abortion rights without a broad, ideological interparty coalition, even with the support of a left-wing party. To reach an equilibrium between doctrinal party commitments and an extensive – usually nondoctrinal – interparty consensus seems to be the touchstone of political negotiations on pro-abortion rights.

As indicated by these three lessons, the best scenario for confronting conservatives is a combination of favorable vertical, horizontal, and intermediary dimensions in the nested networks.

5.1 Exploring the Heuristic Value of the Analytical Model

The Mexican and Brazilian cases go some way in showing how feminists were able to counter conservative attacks. While the Mexico case demonstrates the importance of the vertical dimension, the Brazil case reveals the significance of the horizontal one. Both cases reveal the trade-offs between doctrinal and nondoctrinal agendas and between enabling and blocking results.

The question remains as to how our model holds up if replicated in extreme cases comprising a completely positive or negative coordination of the horizontal and vertical dimensions (see Table 2). Although a proper answer to this question exceeds the scope of this Element, we can explore some possibilities for future research. The recent approval of the IVE law in Argentina may offer the most promising example of positive synergy between the dimensions analyzed in this Element.

40 See the paradigmatic case of Nicaragua in Latin America (Meza and Tatagiba, 2016).

Table 2 Countries by feminist network dimensions*

Vertical dimension	Horizontal dimension	
	More*	**Less**
More	Argentina**	Mexico
Less	Brazil	***

* More implies that feminism is more coordinated within the particular dimension. Less signifies the opposite. More or less implies a comparative relative (not absolute) measurment among countries.

** This is considered as an explorative case analysis

*** One country of Central America (Guatemala) could be located in this cell. Due to the complex control variables needed to include these cases (as the army conflict) and the scope of this Element, we leave the exploration of these cases for future exercises.

Several studies agree on the existence of strong connections between the subdimensions of intersectional, trans, and queer identities within the pro-choice feminist coalition in Argentina (Ciriza, 2013; Sutton and Borland, 2013; Brown, 2020). In particular, Sutton and Borland (2013) offer a detailed analysis of the framing of abortion rights by a remarkable connecting organization, the National Women's Meetings (Encuentro Nacional de Mujeres; referred to as Encuentros), for more than twenty years. Studying Encuentros "reveals aspects of the ongoing development of a broad-based women's movement for abortion rights in Argentina," where the "grassroots, plural and horizontal character of Encuentros facilitates the expression of diverse viewpoints" (Sutton and Borland 2013: 196). By achieving plurality, the Argentinians were able to increase public support for legal abortion, a goal that Brazilian feminists continuously pursue in the face of conservative's growing influence in public opinion. As Di Marco (2000) has pointed out, Argentinian feminists and popular (working class and poor) women's organizations developed a deep affinity, which boosted an intersectional network and prompted a process of "queering abortion rights," incorporating trans-inclusive language into the newly passed abortion rights bill – for instance, referring to "people with the capacity to gestate" without erasing the central role of women (Sutton and Borland, 2018: 11). This equilibrium was the result of an abortion campaign that bridged solidarities between the LGBT+ community and feminists (Bellucci, 2015).

Concerning the vertical and intermediary dimensions, social movements in Argentina, similarly to those in Brazil, actively participated in the democratization process. However, women and feminists in Argentina were able to develop a broad alliance with different ideologically committed parties to pursue political equality. In 1991, they achieved the "30 percent quota law," later followed by the parity law in 2017, which substantially increased the number of women in Congress and political parties. In addition, they have built an extensive presence in the judiciary and, most recently, in the executive, gaining the public support of the president, who presented the bill in Congress (Rodriguez Gustá, 2019).[41] Their presence across the three branches of government was complemented by a country-wide feminist coalition, geographically dispersed throughout the subnational territory and reaching populations and organizations of marginalised women. Due to the strength and stability of these connections, Argentinian feminists overcame the constraints of federalism and the pressure of local elites (Franceschet, 2011), successfully blocking conservative reactions – in the face of Catholic influence and the pope's opposition – (Sutton and Borland, 2013: 195–196) and enabling a resounding triumph in the legalization of abortion on December 30, 2020. In sum, the Argentinian pro-choice network clearly reflects a nested network strongly connected across the various dimensions of our analytical model. In doing so, this network shows an extraordinary blocking and enabling capacity with regard to abortion.

Our exploration of the disputes between feminists and conservatives regarding abortion rights provides various lessons for scholars who study feminism in particular, and social movements in general, but may also be helpful for feminist practitioners. From a relational point of view, cooperative pluralism is an ingredient that strengthens feminism, and the relationship with state institutions a factor that facilitates confronting conservative countermovements more effectively. Moreover, we recognize the crucial role of political parties in facing these challenges. Finally, in this section, we offer a very brief glimpse into the heuristic possibilities of our analytic model for other cases. Our initial exploration augurs well for our constructed relational model. Future research should complement this exercise by exploring each dimension separately or, if possible, by creating comprehensive comparative indices. In any event, lessons learned from the Brazil and Mexico cases show that it is worth the challenge.

[41] Rodriguez-Gustá analyzes how the Argentinian Women's Policy Agency – within the executive – was paradoxically more developed after the Kirshner governments.

References

Abers, R. N. (2020). Institutions, networks and activism inside the state: women's health and environmental policy in Brazil. *Critical Policy Studies*, 15(3), 330–349.

Abers, R. N. & von Bülow, M. (2011). Movimentos sociais na teoria e na prática: como estudar o ativismo através da fronteira entre estado e sociedade? *Sociologias*, 13(28), 52–84.

Abers, R. N. & Keck, M. E. (2013). *Practical Authority: Agency and Institutional Change in Brazilian Water Politics*. Oxford: Oxford University Press.

Abers, R. N., & Tatagiba, L. (2015). Institutional Activism: Mobilizing for Women's Health from Inside the Brazilian Bureaucracy. In F. M. Rossi & M. von Bülow, eds., *Social Movement Dynamics: New Perspectives on Theory and Research from Latin America*. London: Ashgate, 73–101.

Abers, R. N., Serafim, L. & Tatagiba, L. (2014). Repertórios de interação estado-sociedade em um estado heterogêneo: a experiência na Era Lula. *Dados Revista de Ciências Sociais*, 57(2), 325–357.

Abranches, S. (2018). *Presidencialismo de Coalizão: Raízes e Evolução do Modelo político Brasileiro*. São Paulo: Companhia das Letras.

Alarcón, N. (1994). The theoretical subject(s) of this bridge called my back and Anglo-American feminism. In S. Seidman, ed., *The Postmodern Turn: New Perspectives on Social Theory*. Cambridge: Cambridge University Press, 140–152.

Almeida, D. R. (2020). Resiliência institucional: para onde vai a participação nos Conselhos Nacionais de Saúde e dos Direitos da Mulher? *Caderno CRH*, 33, 1–24.

Alvarez, S. (2014). Para além da sociedade civil: reflexões sobre o campo feminista. *Cadernos Pagú*, 43, 13–56.

Alvarez, S. (2019). Feminismos en movimiento, feminismos en protesta. *Revista Punto Género*, 11, 73–102.

Amenta, E., Caren, N., Chiarello, E. & Su, Y. (2010). The political consequences of social movements. *Annual Review of Sociology*, 36(1), 287–307.

Anzaldua, G. (1990). *Making Face, Making Soul/Haciendo Caras: Creative and Critical Perspectives by Feminists of Color*. San Francisco: Aunt Lute Books.

Aziz Nassif, A. (2019). ¿Las Iglesias hasta la Cocina?, *El Universal*. June 25. www.eluniversal.com.mx/articulo/alberto-aziz-nassif/nacion/las-iglesias-hasta-la-cocina.

Banaszak, L. A. (2010). *The Women's Movement Inside and Outside the State*. Cambridge: Cambridge University Press.

Banaszak, L. A. & Whitesell, A. (2017). Inside the state: activism within legislative and governmental agency forums. In H. McCammon, V. Taylor, J. Reger & R. Einwohner, eds., *The Oxford Handbook of US Women's Social Movement Activism*. Oxford: Oxford University Press, 487–506.

Barrancos, D. (2020). *Historia mínima de los feminismos en América Latina*. Mexico City: El Colegio de México.

Barsted, L. (2009). O movimento de mulheres e o debate sobre aborto. In M. I. Baltar da Rocha & R. M. Barbosa, eds., *Aborto no Brasil e Países do Cone Sul: Panorama da Situação e dos Estudos Acadêmicos*. Campinas: Núcleo de Estudos de População – Nepo/Unicamp, 228–256.

Beer, C. (2014). *Measuring Subnational Religious Differences in Mexico: Religion and Gender Equality in Eepemex*. Burlington: University of Vermont.

Beer, C. (2017). Making abortion laws in Mexico: salience and autonomy in the policymaking process. *Comparative Politics*, 50(1), 41–59.

Bellucci, M. (2015). Lo queer como estrategia de lucha abortista (Buenos Aires: 1993–2003). *Herramienta Buenos Aires*, 57, 1–9. https://historiadeunadesobediencia.wordpress.com/2015/11/09/lo-queer-como-estrategia-de-lucha-abortista-buenos-aires-1993-2003/.

Bereni, L. (2021). The women's cause in a field: rethinking the architecture of collective protest in the era of movement institutionalization. *Social Movement Studies*, 20(2), 208–223. https://doi.org/10.1080/14742837.2019.1679107.

Biroli, F. (2016). *Aborto em Debate na Câmara dos Deputados*. Brasília: CFEMEA, Ipas, Observatório de Sexualidade e Política.

Biroli, F. (2018). *Gênero e Desigualdades: Limites da Democracia no Brasil*. São Paulo: Boitempo.

Biroli, F., Machado, M. das D. & Vaggione, J. M. (2020). *Gênero, Neoconservadorismo e Democracia*, 1st ed. São Paulo: Boitempo.

Bogado, M. (2018). Rua. In H. B. Hollanda, ed., *Explosão Feminista*. São Paulo: Companhia das Letras, 23–42.

Bosi, L. (2016). Social movements and interrelated effects: the process of social change in the post-movement lives of provisional IRA volunteers. *Revista Internacional de Sociología*, 74(4), e047. http://dx.doi.org/10.3989/ris.2016.74.4.047.

Brown, J. L. (2020). Del margen al centro: de la construcción del aborto como un problema social al aborto como un derecho (1983–2018). *Cuestiones de Sociología*, 22, 1–18.

Burt, R. S. (2009). *Structural Holes: The Social Structure of Competition*, Cambridge, MA: Harvard University Press.

Butler, J. (2004). *Undoing Gender*. Abingdon: Routledge.

Cabnal, L. (2010). *Feminismos Diversos: El Feminismo Comunitario*. Madrid: ACSUR-Las Segovias.

Careaga, G. & Cruz, S. (2004). *Sexualidades Diversas: Aproximaciones para su Análisis*, Mexico City: Programa Universitario de Estudios de Género y Miguel Ángel Porrúa.

Carlos, E., Dowbor, M. & Albuquerque, M. C. A. (2017). Movimentos sociais e seus efeitos nas políticas públicas: balanço do debate e proposições analíticas. *Civitas – Revista de Ciências Sociais*, 17(2), 360–378.

Carneiro, S. (2001). Rendering feminism blacker: the situation of black women in Latin America from a gender perspective. *Lola Press*, 16(22), 1–6.

Carneiro, S. (2011). *Racismo, Sexismo e Desigualdade no Brasil*. São Paulo: Selo Negro Edições.

Carone, R. R. (2018). A atuação do movimento feminista no legislativo federal: caso da Lei Maria da Penha. *Lua Nova: Revista de Cultura e Política*, 105, 181–216.

Castells, M. (2010). *The Power of Identity*, 2nd ed. Chichester: Chich Wiley-Blackwell.

Ciriza, A. (2013). Sobre el carácter político de la disputa por el derecho al aborto: 30 años de luchas por el derecho a abortar en Argentina. In R. Zurbriggen & C. Anzorena, eds., *El Aborto Como Derecho de las Mujeres: Otra Historia es Posible*. Buenos Aires: Herramienta.

Coacci, T. (2018). *Conhecimento Precário e Conhecimento Contra-público: A Coprodução dos Conhecimentos e dos Movimentos Sociais de Pessoas Trans no Brasil*. Minas Gerais: Universidade Federal de Minas Gerais.

Collier, D. & Levitsky, S. (1997). Democracy with adjectives: conceptual innovation in comparative research. *World Politics*, 49(3), 430–451.

Collier, R. B. & Collier, D. (2002). *Shaping the Political Arena: Critical Junctures, the Labor Movement, and Regime Dynamics in Latin America*, Notre Dame, IN: University of Notre Dame Press.

Correa, S. & Parker, R. (2019). *SexPolitics: Trends and Tensions in the 21st Century – Contextual Undercurrents Volume 2*. Rio de Janeiro: Sexuality Policy Watch.

Crenshaw, K. (1989). Demarginalizing the intersection of race and sex: a black feminist critique of antidiscrimination doctrine, feminist theory and antiracist politics. *University of Chicago Legal Forum*, 1, 139–167.

Cuminao Rojo, C. (2009). Mujeres mapuche: voces y escritura de un posible feminismo indígena. In A. Pequeño, ed., *Participación y Políticas de Mujeres Indígenas en Contextos Latinoamericanos Recientes*. Ecuador: FLACSO-Ecuador, Ministerio de Cultura del Ecuador, 111–124.

Curiel, O., Masson, S. & Falquet, J. (2005). Féminismes dissidents en Amérique latine et aux Caraïbes. *Nouvelles Questions Féministes*, 24(2), 4–13.

Dagnino, E. (2004). Sociedade civil, participação e cidadania: de que estamos falando? In D. Mato, ed., *Políticas de Ciudadanía y Sociedad Civil en Tiempos de Globalización*. Caracas: Universidad Central de Venezuela, 95–110.

Dehesa, R. de la. (2010). *Queering the Public Sphere in Mexico and Brazil: Sexual Rights Movements in Emerging Democracies*, Durham, NC: Duke University Press.

Dehesa, R. de la. (2019). Social medicine, feminism and the politics of population: from transnational knowledge networks to national social movements in Brazil and Mexico. *Global Public Health*, 14(6–7), 803–816.

de Lauretis, T. (1990). Eccentric subjects: feminist theory and historical consciousness. *Feminist Studies*, 16(1), 115–150.

Del Cid Castro, J. A. (2019). *Régimen de Género y Políticas sobre Aborto en Centroamérica los Procesos de Construcción de Agenda en las Asambleas Legislativas*. Mexico City: FLACSO México.

Delgado-Molina, C. (2020). Evangélicos y poder político en México: reconfigurando alianzas y antagonismos. *Encartes*, 3(6), 36–51.

Di Marco, G. (2000). *El Pueblo Feminista: Movimientos Sociales y Lucha de las Mujeres en torno a la Ciudadanía*. Buenos Aires: Biblos.

Diani, M. (1992). The concept of social movement. *The Sociological Review*, 40 (1), 1–25.

Diani, M. & Bison, I. (2004). Organizations, coalitions, and movements. *Theory and Society*, 33(3), 281–309.

Eisenstein, H. (1996). *Inside Agitators: Australian Femocrats and the State*. Philadelphia: Temple University Press.

Enlace Zapatista. (1994). Archivo histórico 5 mayo 1994, *Enlace Zapatista*. https://enlacezapatista.org.mx/1994/05/05/dicen-las-companeras-que-no-piden-clinicas-de-abortos-porque-ni-siquiera-tienen-de-partos/.

Espinosa, Y. (2010). *Aproximaciones Críticas a las Prácticas Teórico-Políticas del Feminismo Latinoamericano*. Buenos Aires: En la Frontera.

Espinoza, C. (2011). Despatriarcalizando el Estado y la sociedad sin permisos. In E. Salguero Carrillo, ed., *Políticas Públicas, Descolonización y Despatriarcalización en Bolivia, Estado Plurinacional*. La Paz: Estado Plurinacional, 77–88.

Facchini, R., do Carmo, I. N. & Pereira Lima, S. (2020). Movimentos feminista, negro e LGBTI no Brasil: sujeitos, teias e enquadramentos. *Educação & Sociedade*, (41), 1–22.

Falleti, T. (2010). *Descentralization and Subnational Politics in Latin America*. Cambridge: Cambridge University Press.

Falleti, T. & Mahoney, J. (2015). The comparative sequential method. In J. Mahoney & K. Thelen, eds., *Advances in Comparative-Historical Analysis*. Cambridge: Cambridge University Press, 211–239.

Fantasia, R. & Stepan-Norris, J. (2004). The labor movement in motion. In D. A. Snow, S. A. Soule & H. Kriesi, eds., *The Blackwell Companion to Social Movements*. Hoboken, NJ: John Wiley & Sons, Ltd., 555–575.

Fanti, F. (2017). Mobilização social e luta por direitos: movimento feminista e a campanha pela descriminalização e legalização do aborto no Brasil, paper presented at VIII Congreso Iberoamericano de Estudios de Género, Buenos Aires, Argentina, 2017.

Fioretos, K. O., Falleti, T. G. & Sheingate, A. D. (2016). *The Oxford Handbook of Historical Institutionalism*. Oxford: Oxford University Press.

Franceschet, S. (2011). Gender policy and state architecture in Latin America. *Politics & Gender*, 7(2), 273–279.

Freeman, L. C. (1977). A set of measures of centrality based on betweenness. *Sociometry*, 40(1), 35–41.

Gargallo, F. (2006). *Las Ideas Feministas Latinoamericanas*. Mexico City: UACM.

Gargallo, F. (2012). *Feminismos Desde Abya Yala: Ideas y Proposiciones de las Mujeres de 607 Pueblos de Nuestra América*. Mexico City: Editorial Corte y Confección.

Goldstone, J. A. (2003). Bridging institutionalized and noninstitutionalized politics. In J. A. Goldstone, ed., *States, Parties, and Social Movements*. Cambridge:Cambridge University Press, 1–24.

Gonzalez, L. (2008). Mulher negra. In E. Larkin, ed., *Guerreiras de Natureza: Mulher Negra, Religiosidade e Ambiente*. São Paulo: Selo Negro, 9–47.

Granovetter, M. (1973). The strength of weak ties. *American Journal of Sociology*, 78 (6), 1360–1380

Gurza Lavalle, A. & von Bülow, M. (2015). Institutionalized brokers and collective actors: different types, similar challenges. In *Social Movement Dynamics: New Perspectives on Theory and Research from Latin America*. Abingdon: Routledge, 157–180.

Gurza Lavalle, A., Carlos, E., Dowbor, M. & Szwako, J. (2018). *Movimentos Sociais e institucionalização: Políticas Sociais, Raça e Gênero no Brasil pós-transição*. Rio de Janeiro: EDUERJ.

Gutterres, A., Vianna, A. & Aguião, S. (2014). Percursos, tensões e possibilidades da participação de movimentos de mulheres e feminista nas políticas governamentais. In J. S. Leite Lopes & B. Heredia, eds., *Movimentos Sociais e Esfera Pública: O Mundo da Participação*. Rio de Janeiro: CBAE.

Halsaa, B. (1998). A strategic partnership for women's policies in Norway. In G. Lycklama à Nijeholt & S. Wieringa, eds., *Women's Movements and Public Policy in Europe, Latin America and the Caribbean*. New York: Garland, 167–189.

Harary, F. (1969) *Graph Theory*. Boston: Addison-Wesley.

Harding, S. (1991). *Whose Science? Whose Knowledge? Thinking from Women's Lives*. New York: Cornell University Press.

Hernández Castillo, R. A. (2016). *Multiple InJustices: Indigenous Women, Law and Political Struggle*. Tucson: University of Arizona Press.

Hernández Castillo, R. A. & Suárez Navaz, L. (2008). *Descolonizando el Feminismo: Teorías y Prácticas desde los Márgenes*. Madrid: Cátedra.

Hochstetler, K. (2011). The politics of environmental licensing: energy projects of the past and future in Brazil. *St Comp Int Dev*, 46, 349–371.

Hochstetler, K. & Keck, M. (2007). *Greening Brazil: Environmental Activism in State and Society*. Durham, NC: Duke University Press.

Holli, A. M. (2008). Feminist triangles: a conceptual analysis. *Journal of Representative Democracy*, 44(2), 169–185.

Hooks, B. (2017). *El Feminismo es para todo el Mundo*. Madrid: Traficante de sueños.

Htun, M. & Weldon, S. L. (2018). *The Logics of Gender Justice: State Action on Women's Rights Around the World*. Cambridge: Cambridge University Press.

INEGI. (2021). *Censo Población y Vivienda 2020*, INEGI, viewed March 2, 2021.

Jeffreys, S. (2003). *Unpacking Queer Politics: A Lesbian Feminist Perspective*. Cambridge: Polity Press.

Jessop, B. (2015). *State Power*. London: Polity Press.

Kantola, J. (2006). *Feminists Theorize the State*. New York: Palgrave Macmillan.

Keck, M. E. & Sikkink, K. (1998). *Activists beyond Borders: Advocacy Networks in International Politics*. Ithaca: Cornell University Press.

Kingdom, John W. (1995). *Agendas, Alternatives, and Public Policies*. 2nd ed. New York: Harper Collins.

Korol, C. (2016). *Somos Tierra, Semilla, Rebeldía: Mujeres, Tierra y Territorios en América Latina*. Buenos Aires: GRAIN, Acción por la Biodiversidad y América Libre.

Labastida Martín Del Campo, J. & Leyva, M. A. L. (2004). México: una transición prolongada (1988–1996/97). *Revista Mexicana de Sociología*, 66 (4), 749–806.

Lacerda, M. (2018). *Neoconservadorismo de Periferia: Articulação Familista, Primitiva e Neoliberal na Câmara dos Deputados*. Rio de Janeiro: State University of Rio de Janeiro.

Lamas, M. (2015). *El Largo Camino Hacia la ILE: Mi Versión de los Hechos*. Mexico City: UNAM.

López, J. (2020). Aborto, contramovilización y estrategias de comunicación contra la expansión de derechos en México. *Revista Interdisciplinaria de Estudios de Género de El Colegio de México*, 6, e621. https://estudiosdegenero.colmex.mx/index.php/eg/article/view/621/pdf.

Löwy, M. (2004). Le concept d'affinité élective chez Max Weber. *Archives de Sciences Sociales des Religions*, 127 (July–September). https://doi.org/10.4000/assr.1055.

Lozano, B. (2010). El feminismo no puede ser uno porque las mujeres somos diversas: aportes a un feminismo negro decolonial desde la experiencia de las mujeres negras del Pacífico Colombiano. *La Manzana de la Discordia*, 5(2), 7–24. https://doi.org/10.25100/lamanzanadeladiscordia.v5i2.1516.

Lugones, M. (2011). Hacia un feminismo descolonial. *La Manzana de la Discordia*, 6(2), 105–119.

Luna, N. (2014). Aborto no Congresso Nacional: o enfrentamento de atores religiosos e feministas em um Estado laico. *Revista Brasileira de Ciência Política*, (14), 83–109.

Mainwaring, S., Power, T. & Bizarro, F. (2018). The uneven institutionalization of a party system: Brazil. In S. Mainwaring, ed., *Party Systems in Latin America: Institutionalization, Decay, and Collapse*. Cambridge: Cambridge University Press, 164–200.

Mann, M. (1984). The autonomous power of the state: its origins, mechanisms and results. *European Journal of Sociology*, 25(2), 185–213.

Mariano, R. & Biroli, F. (2012). O debate sobre aborto na Câmara dos Deputados (1991–2014): posições e vozes das mulheres parlamentares. *Cadernos Pagu*, (10), 1–38.

Martello, L. (2018). O debate sobre legalização do aborto e a inclusão de diferenças nas 3ª e 4ª Conferências Nacionais de Políticas para Mulheres: direito ao corpo e feminismos jovens. In *Quem são as Mulheres das Políticas para as Mulheres no Brasil: Expressões Feministas nas Conferências Nacionais de Políticas para as Mulheres*. Porto Alegre: Zouk, 211–255.

Martinez Medina, D. (2010). *Redes de Política Pública y Construcción de Agenda de Género en el Legislativo Mexicano (1997–2009)*. Mexico City: FLACSO México .

Matos, M. & Alvarez, S. (2018). *Quem são as Mulheres das Políticas para as Mulheres no Brasil: o Feminismo Estatal Participativo Brasileiro*. Porto Alegre: Editora Zouk.

McBride Stetson, D., ed. (2001). *Abortion Politics, Women's Movements, and the Democratic State: A Comparative Study of State Feminism, Abortion*

Politics, Women's Movements, and the Democratic State. Oxford: Oxford University Press.

McBride, D. & Mazur, A. G. (2010). *The Politics of State Feminism Innovation in Comparative Research*. Philadelphia: Temple University Press.

Medeiros, J. (2019). Do feminismo popular ao feminismo periférico: mudanças estruturais em contapúblicos da Zona Leste de São Paulo. *Novos Rumos Sociológicos*, 7(11), 300–335.

Medeiros, J. & Fanti, F. (2017). Recent changes in the Brazilian feminist movement: the emergence of new collective actors. In J. P. Ferrero, A. Natalucci and L. Tatagiba, eds., *Socio-political Dynamics within the Crisis of the Left: Argentina and Brazil*. London: Rowman & Littlefield, 221–241.

Mendoza, B. (2014). La cuestión de la colonialidad del género. In *Ensayos de crítica feminista en nuestra América*. Mexico City: Herder, 45–71.

Meyer, D. S. & Staggenborg, S. (1996). Movements, countermovements, and the structure of political opportunity. *American Journal of Sociology*, 101(6), 1628–1660.

Meza, H. and Tatagiba, L. (2016). Movimentos sociais e partidos políticos: as relações entre o movimento feminista e o sistema de partidos na Nicarágua (1974–2012). *Opinião Pública*, 22(2), 350–384.

Miguel, L. F., Biroli, F. & Mariano, R. (2017). O direito ao aborto no debate legislativo brasileiro: a ofensiva conservadora na Câmara dos Deputados. *Opinião Pública*, 23(1), 230–260.

Miyares, A. (2017). Las trampas conceptuales de la reacción neoliberal: «relativismo», «elección», «diversidad» e «identidad». *Revista Europea de Derechos Fundamentales*, 29, 117–132.

Mohanty, C. T. & Russo & Torres, L. (1991). *Third World Women and the Politics of Feminism*. Bloomington: Indiana University Press.

Nahmias-Wolinsky, Y. (2004). *Models, Numbers, and Cases: Methods for Studying International Relations*. Michigan: University of Michigan Press.

Norris P. (1997) Choosing electoral systems: proportional, majoritarian and mixed systems. *International Political Science Review*, 18(3), 297–312.

Ortiz Ortega, A. O. (2019). *Si los Hombres se Embarazaran, ¿el Aborto seria Legal?*. Mexico City: EDAMEX.

Pacari, N. (2004). *La Participación Política de la Mujer Indígena en el Parlamento Ecuatoriano. Una Tarea Pendiente*. Stockholm: Institute for Democracy and Electoral Assistance.

Paradis, C. & Matos, M. (2013). Los feminismos latinoamericanos y su compleja relación con el Estado: debates actuales. *Íconos Revista de Ciencias Sociales*, (43), 91–107.

Paredes, J. & Guzmán, A. (2014). *El tejido de la rebeldía, ¿qué es el feminismo comunitario?* La Paz: Mujeres Creando Comunidad.

Perez Flores, E. & Amuchastegui Herrera, A. (2012). Interrupción legal del embarazo: reescribiendo la experiencia del aborto en los hospitales públicos del Distrito Federal. *Género y Salud en cifras*, 10(1), 21–30.

Pérez Guadalupe, J. L. (2017). *Entre Dios y el César: El Impacto Político de los Evangélicos en el Perú y América Latina*. Lima: Konrad-Adenauer-Stiftung and Instituto de Estudios Social Cristianos (IESC).

Pierson, P. (2011). *Politics in Time: History, Institutions, and Social Analysis*. Princeton: Princeton University Press.

Pinto, C. R. (2010). Feminismo, história e poder. *Revista de Sociologia e Política*, 18(36), 15–23.

Piscopo, J. M. & Walsh, D. M. (2020). Introduction: symposium backlash and the future of feminism. *Signs Journal of Women in Culture and Society*, 45(2), 265–278.

Pou Giménez, F. (2014). The new Mexican constitutional remedy ("amparo") and the protection of rights: neither so new nor so protective? *Anuario de Derechos Humanos*, 10, 91–103.

Prieto, M., Cuminao, C., Flores, A., Maldonado, G. & Pequeño, A. (2005). Las mujeres indígenas y la búsqueda del respeto. In M. Prieto, ed., *Mujeres Ecuatorianas, entre la Crisis y las Oportunidades 1990–2004*. Quito: CONAMU, FLACSO-Ecuador, UNFPA, UNIFEM, 155–196.

Queiroz, C. (2019). Fé pública: pesquisadores buscam compreender crescimento evangélico no Brasil. *Revista FAPESP*, 20(286), 12–19.

Reuterswärd, C. (2018). Mobilizing for mortal sin? Social movements and the struggle over abortion policy in sub-national Mexico. Paper prepared for the Annual Meeting of the Latin American Studies Association (LASA), Barcelona, Spain May 26.

Richards, P. (2002). Expandir el concepto de ciudadanía de las mujeres: La visión de pueblo y la representación de las mujeres mapuche en SERNAM. In *Impactos y desafíos de las crisis internacionales*. Santiago de Chile: FLACSO-Chile, 267–297.

Rios, F., Perez, O. & Ricoldi, A. (2018). Interseccionalidade nas mobilizações do Brasil contemporâneo. *Lutas Sociais*, 22(40), 36–51.

Rocha, C. (2020). Cristianismo ou conservadorismo? O caso do movimento antiaborto no Brasil. *Revista TOMO*, 36, 43–78.

Rodrigues, C. & Gonçalves Freitas, V. (2021). Ativismo feminista negro no Brasil: do movimento de mulheres negras ao feminismo interseccional. *Revista Brasileira de Ciência Política*, (34), 1–54.

Rodriguez Gustá, A. L. (2019). Women's policy agencies and government ideology: the divergent roads of Argentina and Brazil 2003–2019. Paper presented at the Conference Feminisms and Conservatisms, FLACSO Mexico, Mexico City, September 19–20.

Roggeband, C. & Krizsán, A. (2020). Democratic backsliding and the backlash against women's rights: understanding the current challenges for feminist politics. UN Women discussion paper, 35.

Saunders, C. (2007). Using social network analysis to explore social movements: a relational approach. *Social Movement Studies*, 6, 227–243.

Schedler, A. (2010). Democracy's past and future: authoritarianism's last line of defense. *Journal of Democracy*, 21(1), 69–80.

Seawright, J. & Gerring, J. (2008). Case selection techniques in case study research: a menu of qualitative and quantitative options. *Political Research Quarterly*, 61(2), 294–308.

Segato, R. L. (2014). Las nuevas formas de la guerra y el cuerpo de las mujeres. *Sociedade e Estado*, 29(2), 341–371.

Sierra, M. T. (2008). Mujeres indígenas, justicia y derechos: los retos de una justicia intercultural. *Revista Íconos*, (31), 15–26.

Silva, M. K. & Pereira, M. M. (2020). Movimentos e contramovimentos sociais: o caráter relacional da conflitualidade social. *Revista Brasileira de Sociologia – RBS*, 8(20), 26–49.

Sorj, B. (2016). Connecting economic and social policy: new approaches to gender equality. *Global Social Policy*, 16(1), 105–108.

Sorj, B. (2018). As veteranas ou um sinal de alerta sobre uma memória não escrita. In H. B. Hollanda, ed., *Explosão Feminista*. São Paulo: Companhia das Letras, 431–438.

Soto Fregoso, M. A. (2019). La auto adscripción de género en el registro de candidaturas a concejalías en el estado de Oaxaca. In C. R. Eguiarte Mereles & M. Pérez Cepeda, eds., *Desafíos de la Democracia Incluyente: Colección Instituto Electoral del Estado de Querétaro*. Mexico City: IEEQ, 101–121.

SPM (Secretaria Especial de Políticas para Mulheres). (2016). Legados da 4ª Conferência Nacional de Políticas para Mulheres em Imagens. Brasília: ONU Mulheres.

Sutton, B. & Borland, E. (2013). Framing abortion rights in Argentina's Encuentros Nacionales de Mujeres. *Feminist Studies*, 39(1), 194–234.

Sutton, B. & Borland, E. (2018). Queering abortion rights: notes from Argentina. *Culture, Health & Sexuality*, 20(12), 1378–1393.

Szwako, J. (2014). O mau desempenho de Lugo: gênero, religião e contramovimento na última destituição presidencial paraguaia. *Opinião Pública*, 20(1), 132–155.

Tarrés, M. L. (2006). Nuevos nudos y desafíos en las prácticas feministas: los Institutos de las Mujeres en México. *Revista Enfoques: Ciencia Política y Administración*, (5), 5–27.

Tarrés Barraza, M. L. & Zaremberg, G. (2014). Conclusiones. In S. López Estrada, E. Maier, M. L. Tarrés Barraza & G. Zaremberg, eds., *15 Años de Políticas de Igualdad: Los Alcances, los Dilemas y los Retos*. Mexico City: COLEF, El Colegio de México, FLACSO México.

Teles, M. A. de A. (1999). *Breve História do Feminismo no Brasil*. São Paulo: Brasiliense.

Tilly, C. (1995). Contentious repertoires in Great Britain, 1758–1834. In: M. Traugott, ed., *Repertoires and Cycles of Collective Action*. Durham, NC: Duke University Press, 15–42.

Torres Pacheco, M. G. A. (2008). *¿Dónde Inician las Leyes? Poder Ejecutivo y Poder Legislativo en el Proceso de Formulación de la Ley General de Acceso de las Mujeres a una Vida Libre de Violencia*. Mexico City: FLACSO México.

Valcárcel, A. (2019). *Ahora, Feminismo: Cuestiones Candentes y Frentes Abiertos*. Madrid: Cátedra.

Varela, N. (2019). *Feminismo 4.0: La Cuarta Ola*. Madrid: Ediciones B.

Vargas, V. (2008). *Feminismos en América Latina su Aporte a la Política y a la Democracia*. Lima: Universidad Nacional de San Marcos.

Vargas, V. & Wieringa, S. (1998). The triangle of empowerment: processes and actors in the making of public policy for women. In G. Lycklama à Nijeholt, V. Vargas & S. Wieringa, eds., *Women's Movements and Public Policy in Europe, Latin America and the Caribbean*. New York: Garland, 3–23.

Waiselfisz, J. J. (2015). *Mapa da Violência 2015: Homicídio de Mulheres no Brasil*, 1st ed., Brasília: OPAS, OMS, ONU Mulheres, SPM, FLACSO.

Wasserman, S. & Faust, K. (1994). *Social Network Analysis: Methods and Applications*, Cambridge: Cambridge University Press.

Wilkinson, A. (2021). Gender as a death threat to the family: how the "security frame" shapes anti-gender activism in Mexico. International Feminist Journal of Politics, 23(4), 535–557. https://doi.org/10.1080/14616742.2021.1957974.

Woodward, A. E. (2004). *Building Velvet Triangles: Gender and Informal Governance, Informal Governance in the European Union*. Cheltenham: Edward Elgar Publishing.

Zaremberg, G. (2007). Alpargatas y libros: un análisis comparado de los estilos de gestión social del Consejo Provincial de la Mujer (Provincia de Bs. As, Argentina) y el Servicio Nacional de la Mujer (Chile). In G. Zaremberg, ed.,

Políticas Sociales y Género, Tomo I: La Institucionalización. Mexico City: FLACSO.

Zaremberg, G. (2009). *¿Cuánto y para qué?: los derechos políticos de las mujeres desde la óptica de la representación descriptiva y sustantiva*. Mexico City: Tribunal Federal Electoral de la Federación.

Zaremberg, G. & Guzmán Lucero, Á. F. (2019). Aborto, movimientos y femocracias: un análisis relacional. *Revista Mexicana de Sociología*, 81 (1), 145–177.

Zaremberg, G., Guarneros-Meza, V. & Gurza Lavalle, A. (2017). *Intermediation and Representation in Latin America: Actors and Roles Beyond Elections*, London: Palgrave Macmillan.

Acknowledgements

We thank the CNPQ – National Council for Scientific and Technological Development for the funding of the Project, Process N. 426882/2016–4, and for the Research Productivity Fellowship. The Research Group RESOCIE and the Political Science Postgraduate Program from the University of Brasilia. In Mexico, we appreciate the support of FLACSO. We are also grateful to Rebecca Abers, Adrián Gurza Lavalle, Constanza Tabbush and the participants of the Seminar "Feminisms and Conservatism in Latin America," held in Mexico City on September 2019.

Cambridge Elements

Politics and Society in Latin America

Political Studies, *Latin American Politics & Society*, *Social Forces*, and *World Development*, among other journals, and his co-authored book, *Root-Cause Regulation: Labor Inspection in Europe and the Americas*.

About the Series

Latin American politics and society are at a crossroads, simultaneously confronting serious challenges and remarkable opportunities that are likely to be shaped by formal institutions and informal practices alike. The Elements series on Politics and Society in Latin America offers multidisciplinary and methodologically pluralist contributions on the most important topics and problems confronted by the region.

Cambridge Elements ☰

Politics and Society in Latin America

Elements in the series

Understanding Institutional Weakness
Daniel M. Brinks, Steven Levitsky, Maria Victoria Murillo

Neo-extractivism in Latin America
Maristella Svampa

The Politics of Transitional Justice in Latin America
Ezequiel A. Gonzalez-Ocantos

The Politics of LGBTQ Rights Expansion in Latin America and the Caribbean
Javier Corrales

The Distributive Politics of Environmental Protection in Latin America and the Caribbean
Isabella Alcañiz, Ricardo A. Gutiérrez

The Circuit of Detachment in Chile
Kathya Araujo

Beyond 'Plata O Plomo'
Gustavo Duncan

The Post-Partisans
Carlos Meléndez

The Political Economy of Segmented Expansion: Latin American Social Policy in the 2000s
Camila Arza, Rossana Castiglioni, Juliana Martínez Franzoni, Sara Niedzwiecki, Jennifer Pribble, Diego Sánchez-Ancochea

Feminism In Latin America
Gisela Zaremberg, Debora Rezende de Almeida

A full series listing is available at: www.cambridge.org/PSLT

Printed in the USA
CPSIA information can be obtained
at www.ICGtesting.com
CBHW070939270324
5932CB00005B/279

9 781108 825962